LANDFALL 238

November 2019

Editor Emma Neale
Founding Editor Charles Brasch (1909–1973)

Cover: Nigel Brown, *Sea Protect*, 2018–19, acrylic and beads on canvas, 1350 x 800 mm.

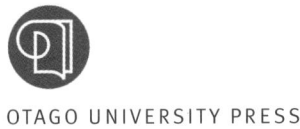

OTAGO UNIVERSITY PRESS

CONTENTS

The Landfall Review

JENNY BORNHOLDT

Kathleen Grattan Award for Poetry 2019 Judge's Report

'Sinking Lessons', by **Philip Armstrong**, is an accomplished, engaging collection of poems that displays literary skill and a sharp intelligence at work.

Armstrong's poems are shapely and interesting—they're written by someone who thinks about how words go together, how a line feels. Craft is what I'm talking about. That old-fashioned word—spending time and care on making something that will last.

We know that work has happened to these poems—not that they feel 'worked on', but that there's thought and a skill with language propelling them forwards. The poems range easily from the personal to wider issues like the environment and history. There's great affection for life of all kinds—human and the natural world—coupled with an awareness of the fragility of existence. This is a person who looks and sees the way 'The morning easterly scrapes and scrapes/the torn-up estuary tide ...' About a homeless person, he writes: 'His heart maketh a noise in him.' It's a noise we should be hearing and taking notice of.

In a similar way, we should be paying attention to larger concerns such as the warming of the planet. In one poem Armstrong re-animates Frankenstein. The bolted creature is reborn; midwived by the hot breath of a musk ox in a warming Arctic. What emerges is an unsettling, perfectly judged metaphor for what will be unleashed if action is not taken now on climate change.

I admire the way the poet tackles history. In a final sequence he imaginatively reconstructs events that led to the wrecking of the HMS *Orpheus* on the Manukau Bar in 1863, en route from Sydney to Auckland. Inaccurate charts—inaccurate for the simple reason that seabeds are constantly changing (in this case, land clearance led to runoff that altered the seabed).

There's a lot of weather, there are communication systems, coordinates and ways of mapping that fit well with the way the poet charts his own past. The overlaps and convergences. I like the way time behaves in his poems— it's fluid and strange. These are poems awash with memory and history. In one, a dog dodging traffic recalls a pair of dogs brought to Dunedin on a boat in 1851. The animals escape and head for the hills, frightening late-night walkers. In another poem we have migrating eels 'refusing/to forget the places their parents knew. Generation's/generations …'

There's a lot of water also—mostly ocean and all it brings with it and carries away. And this is linked to history, for example, the dredge working Otago Harbour; the then and now of tides, the seabed and the city.

A great sense of movement pervades—through time, by water, in memory—and at the same time a feeling of these poems being embedded in landscape, peoples and history. All is handled sensitively and imaginatively, and I'm very pleased to select Philip Armstrong's 'Sinking Lessons' to win the Kathleen Grattan Award for Poetry 2019.

The following submissions (alphabetical order by title) were shortlisted: 'Dismantle' by **Semira Davis**; 'Every Way of Water' by **Robyn Maree Pickens**; 'Magical Māori Mystery Tour of Wellington' by **Debbie Broughton**; 'The Seed Drill' by **Ben Egerton**; and 'Unseasoned Campaigner' by **Janet Newman**.

I congratulate all of the above on their manuscripts. A number were outstanding— deeply embedded in thought and experience—and I'm sorry there can be only one 'winner', but I'm certain that a number of the shortlisted manuscripts will be published.

EMMA NEALE

Landfall Essay Competition 2019 Judge's Report

The essay competition this year might have drawn fewer entries (64; well down on last year's 91) but it was far more gruelling terrain to cover as a judge. There were several memoirs of cancer, or biographies of parental cancer; the subjects tended to dwell on darkness: ranging from addiction, self-harm, mental illness, the Christchurch mosque attacks, to the housing crisis. The submissions were almost uniformly haunted, troubled. Essays that emanated joy, or delighted in acquiring knowledge, were rare. For this reason, I want to fly a bright pennant to one entry, 'Themes and Variations: The 9½-fingered pianist', by Tui Bevan, on the strength not just of its relaxed style, but also for its celebration of intimacy and its wryly affectionate acknowledgment of a piano as the third member of a marriage. Although it wasn't shortlisted, it did offer welcome respite from the darkness for a few thousand words.

For the winning essays, I sought prose that had finesse yet also the utmost clarity. When there are around 60 other voices asking to be heard, ornate, laden, complexly reticulated syntax, with metaphors nested inside similes folded inside obscure metonymy, quickly seems self-indulgent—even if the subject is of topical political relevance or has the supposed 'VIP pass' of tackling high or canonised culture. I wanted work that was intelligent yet direct and that also offered buoyancy—even if this uplift was not in subject matter or resolution, but through the energy of the prose rhythms or the precision and surprise of the descriptive language.

The highly commended and commended essays ranged in topic from the joys and distress of GP work in South Auckland; to two works on how our sense of language, story, time and parenthood are altered by the anxiety of trying to absorb the reality of climate crisis; to a spiralling discussion of the virtues of wilderness versus constraint, of wisdom and insight coming from difficulty, all of which hovers around a visit to an owl café in Japan. There was also a caregiver's vivid, frank and compassionate series of portraits of a number of physically or intellectually disabled clients. The mordant irony and dissonance between the supposedly humble yet sneakingly self-congratulatory nationalism of the title, 'Kiwi Made', and the picture of the often hidden, denied or stigmatised in our society, was almost enough on its own to earn this essay its commendation.

All the highly commended and commended essays were of great merit; selecting only a handful from a legion of serious and worthy entrants was a very demanding task.

First Equal
Tobias Buck's 'Exit. Stage Left.' deals with issues of prejudice and bias from the perspective of a man who 'is the colour of cotton candy or pink marshmallows', whose hair is 'definitely platinum', and who as a result, since childhood, experiences a particular kind of labelling: 'It situates you on the edge of the crowd. Casper the Friendly Ghost. Reclusive. A milquetoast. Fauntleroy. Bookish. Effete. Cloistered.' It is full of persuasive visual detail and an ear for the unpleasant reverberations of everyday speech: 'You could get away with anything with a face like that.' 'Jeanette, who cuts my hair, says people would kill for the colour.' His extreme paleness means strangers make knee-jerk assumptions about his political or cultural affiliations. He registers deep discomfort over 'the hierarchy of colour that floats through our culture' yet is also suspicious 'of my own idea of being woke, or anyone else that puts energy into making sure others see them as having arrived'.

I admire the way the essay also effortlessly displays touches of history, pop culture and general knowledge in its discussion of the strange sideways dance of identity. Technically, 'Exit. Stage Left.' executed the bolder parting gesture of the two neck-and-neck first-place essays.

Nina Mingya Powles' 'Tender Gardens' tackles profound, even urgent subject matter with an agility of style and achieves that sweet paradox of an artwork that both allows for pleasure and beauty, yet also tightens the screws on our recognition of various humanitarian or philosophical issues: such as racial prejudice, protecting and nurturing cultural identity and how to make a home in a foreign land. Its careful structure—with sections named as neatly as a conscientious gardener would label seedling varieties in the dark season—helps to make it stand out significantly. So too does its rhapsodic poetic touch, which alights on a wide variety of ideas. The essay moves from so-called casual racism, to measuring the seasons and growing a garden, to the inheritance of knowledge and love, to seeking poetic lineage as a Chinese New Zealander, to the long aftermath of war and enforced migration, to the unconscionable fascistic violence of the Christchurch/Ōtautahi mosque attack, to the deep bond between mother and daughter. In delicate lines it draws links between the innate responses of plants to their environment, and the author's reaction to both thoughtless and deliberately injurious bias.

I found the gently plangent yet provisional ending understated enough to leave a small beat of editorial hesitation, which I felt gave me room to nominate another essay in shared first place.

Third Place

The irreverent, comic style of **Sarah Harpur**'s 'Dead Dads Club' is like the arrival of an unexpectedly proficient circus act in a lonely dustbowl suburb. Fuelled by sharp, authentic sadness and anger, the tone also skewers social expectations, sanctimonious platitudes, and exhortations to stiffen up your stoicism, tighten up your '*she'll be right*' by deliberately over-stating the obvious, mismatching scale of response to the subject matter, offering utterly useless advice, running with hyperbole (and knowingly taking even that too far), exposing the awkward kind of conversational dodge from profound psychic hurt to trivia (fat milk or trim?) that characterises many a supermarket aisle encounter. 'We're not in a note-leaving zeitgeist, but if you absolutely insist on committing suicide, it's only polite. This way, your family can make photocopies of the suicide note and keep one in their wallet, just in case the subject comes up. And it will.' This essay is full of uncomfortable truths and revelations: verbal equivalents of a comb-over flipping up to look electrocuted in the wind, or a pint of beer poured on your head when you've been a total arse. Shockingly refreshing.

Fourth Equal

Joan Fleming's 'Write First, Apologise Later' is a fluent, tumbling, hectic (and yet artfully so) confession and discussion about the rights and responsibilities of the artist. When a friend or fiancé confides trauma or vulnerability, should the artist swear to secrecy, or is anything up for grabs when art transmutes and transforms, and traces the general from the particular? In an intoxicating fusion of content and form, this essay has the immediacy of a friend confessing to secret transgressions; it's so personal in some moments that I felt the same hesitancy over the power of sharing the tale that the writer explores. It hands on that burning burden of *what should I do with this, now that I know it?* In the end its discussions of both troubled intimacy and the role of writing are out-of-body incisive. By this I mean that the writer seems capable of a film director's objectivity on the oddness and warp of her own reactions and relationships. (Ironically, considering her ex-fiancé's role.) The essay's strong poetic language helps it to split the potentially opaque meniscus of narcissism to let the air of wider ethical questions gust through with bracing force.

'The Art and Adventure of Subsistence' by **Jillian Sullivan**
From a childhood strained by domestic violence, to the role that art plays in trying to achieve meaningful work, this gently probing essay is both limber and lyrical in its efforts to describe the complex web of achieving full mental or psychological health when other basic human needs are in a tenuous limbo. With remarkably graceful restraint it expresses the deep frustrations in dealing with the Department of Work and Income in the aftermath of personal crisis and the arduous transitions of divorce. Its hard-earned wisdom read like a balm after a swathe of essays in this intake that dwelt in the long dark night of the soul and that, distressingly, couldn't quite find their way to a place of health. The quiet optimism, the understated argument for community and the stylistic ease of this essay offer the very solace that the author, in her toughest moments, clearly mined deep to source and then carefully craft for herself.

Highly Commended
Ingrid Horrocks ('Where We Swim'); **Himali McInnes** ('This Place'); **Derek Schulz** ('Kiwi Made').

Commended
Justine Jungersen-Smith ('Half Sugar Half Sand'); **Amy Brown** ('To Hold in the Palm of the Hand').

Exit. Stage Left.

I'm fair-skinned at best. And blond. But not the Aryan tanned-Adonis type. Most of my freckles have been too shy to join up. Got that Irish tan. That Kiwi tan. That sweet, sweet ruddy pallor. Chances are good I'm whiter than you.

Easily sunburnt, I could pass for Swiss or Swedish. I've been shouted at in Danish by people who think I'm ignoring them. But this isn't about that. At least, I think it's not. It's about being slightly, but definitely, pink.

Imagine being the colour of candyfloss or marshmallows. I appear strawberry-flavoured. It's a hard thing to complain about—I'm clearly delicious. People can tell when I'm getting worked up, angry or embarrassed. You can see my frustrations. You can see if I'm drunk. It's obvious when I blush.

'He's turning red! Look at him!'

Which used to make me further embarrassed, less prone to speaking out or being too vulnerable or emotional in public.

Both my parents are redheads. Dad was coppery-blond. Mum's hair was auburn red like an Irish setter. Dad still calls her Rust. Her great-grandmother Inez was born on Long Hope in the Orkney Islands, a way north of Scotland. She had such pale blue eyes they photographed as white. Startling. Ghostly. I read that it happens when generations live by the sea. There's a touch of something Viking or Celtic about it. Makes me think of distant islands, all in a chain ... the cold sparkling shores of Oban. The windswept Shetlands. Uist, Benbecula, Barra, Rùm. The Outer Hebrides. The Northern Isles.

Inez had a cousin, Abraham, who one day was washed from the black rocks while fishing. Never to be seen again.

Dad's colouring is something else, something from Northern Ireland and tin miners in Cornwall. Along the Devon coast. Penzance. Fair-skinned, fair-haired, rosy-cheeked. There's a connection to Lille, to Île-de-France and Brittany. Perhaps a touch Norman.

In New Zealand I grew up mostly with white kids around me. Not as pink or pale as me, but still white. My blondness, my rosy shade—they work in your favour as a child. Growing up in the 1980s I looked angelic, apparently. Cherubic even. Blue-eyed. A Milkybar kid. Heavy on the milk. Innocent. Cute. A golden boy.

'You could get away with anything with a face like that.'

When you're a poster child for some utopian dream you don't understand, you feel special. You feel 'good' somehow, but you haven't done anything to deserve it. Something from the communal psyche gets ascribed to you and you don't know why. It sits uneasily.

I've seen pictures of myself from back then. My chin tilted up, beaming. A bowl cut that reflects so much light it causes lens flares on the camera. I am the blondest, pinkest kid in every school photo, as if I've been picked out with a limelight. Overexposed.

Jeanette, who cuts my hair, says people would kill for the colour.

'Definitely platinum,' she says, measuring it with her fingers.

'It'll go dark one day. Dirty blond,' says another. 'That's what it does.'

In the summer of 1991 the Mongrel Mob had a New Year's Eve party in the public domain opposite my parents' bach. Short on bathrooms, they politely knocked on the door. For a few days they'd come over in two or threes. While waiting they'd sit on the couch with Dad and me and watch the Gulf War on TV.

It was the first televised war; cameras on Tomahawk cruise missiles showed black-and-white crosshairs flying down the streets of Kuwait. They zoomed down alleyways, around corners towards nondescript doors. Almost a video game, it was war by remote. Exotic. Across distant seas but, for the first time, brought close up, fed straight into homes. Unlike anything before, it made for a weird kind of reality show. The stakes couldn't have been higher.

I got so familiar with the gang being in and out of the bach that one hot day, seeing them riding along the beachfront, past the surf life-saving tower—a mass of chromed bikes, tattoos and black leather—I pedalled my red BMX into the centre of the group. For a few minutes they let me ride among them. People laughed. I thought it was funny. It could have gone another way. A little blond anomaly amidst all that formidable metal gleaming in the summer sun. I was grinning ear to ear, proud as punch.

As I got older the way I looked got trickier. It seemed to pick up baggage as it rolled out into the world. My pink hue was less cute, its effect riskier and more complex.

At high school there's usually a nickname for the blond kid: Snowy, Bluey, Old Man. Old before your time. My brothers had theirs too. The oldest probably got the worst: Petit Cochon—Little Pig. The tradition at my school was to use the specific name of a real blond and pale kid from a decade earlier: I got John Boore. I never knew him but he hadn't been much liked; no doubt resentful at being singled out. That's the way it goes, though: the more you rail against a nickname the more it sticks. The urge to find a pigeonhole, to box up, name and categorise a person is universal. As with the mythical Bed of Procrustes, whatever there is about you that doesn't fit will just be abbreviated.

The names for pale kids had a pejorative element. You just knew, somehow, in terms of status on the social ladder that being this luminous shade was no advantage. Tanned skin speaks of health, holidays, pleasure. Too pale is the opposite. A Boo Radley. That kid in *Sixteen Candles*. Pale in comparison. It situates you on the edge of the crowd. Casper the Friendly Ghost. Reclusive. A milquetoast. Fauntleroy. Bookish. Effete. Cloistered.

The visibility made me self-conscious. You reflect more light. You attract attention and make an easy target. It's a peculiarity, like being very tall. People can pick you out in a crowd. You get called out for it.

'You're not an albino,' one girl says. Slowly. After some consideration. Before turning her attention to another boy.

I can tell you about the embarrassment. I didn't like mirrors. I wanted to fit in. When I was thirteen I emptied a bottle of tanning lotion all over my legs and headed out to town to show them off. Thought that was cool.

Plus, that choir boy look is a thing apparently. As a kid I'd been lured away once or twice while playing at a park, before Mum could locate me. As a teen I'd get the odd hand on the knee under a table. A breathy, hushed whisper. A friend's stepdad pushing porn and beer at you, asking when you'll come over by yourself. At university I'd be regularly propositioned if out late at night. Caught a bit off guard, I'd be stopped and furtively questioned.

'You alone? Where are you going?'

But, like I say, who am I to complain? People have much worse to contend with. Like the Pink Panther on Saturday morning cartoons, or Snagglepuss with his tuxedo collar and fancy cuffs, you learnt a certain footwork. You learn to make light of it, to make light of being light. With avoidance humour, almost theatrical, you dance around the subject. Head off script. Do your best to step around a subject that might leave you easily categorised or written off. Remove yourself as a target. Make it appear natural. Exit. Stage left.

Once, when I was fourteen, at a petrol station in the town where I grew up, I was standing on the forecourt waiting for a friend inside when a ute rolled up. Three, maybe four teenagers were on the back. Older than me. Bigger than me. While the driver filled up they nodded in my direction. I didn't know why. I looked at my feet and wished my friend would hurry.

One of the boys stood up, facing me. He extended his arm, just above shoulder height. Then they all stood and did the same. Arms out. Palms down.

They kept looking. Waiting for me to respond.

MTV was established and became a massive screen presence through the early 1990s. Breakdancing was the height of coolness. When a music video wanted to show it had credibility or flair, when the beat dropped and the chorus peaked, for a few seconds breakdancers would appear, flipping, spinning and worming across neon, graffiti-sprayed stage sets.

I immediately got out every available book on the subject from our very small-town library. I would cycle thirty minutes to get there, then return with my precious cargo to sit under the dining table and read. Large-format hardbacks had sequences of black-and-white photos showing how to do the robot. I would warm a cushion in front of the heater to practise my head spins on. In the living room I'd push back the couch and coffee table and break away. I had my own piece of cardboard. I would put on shows for family members.

At the wedding reception of an uncle who lived on the Kāpiti coast, a hired crew of breakdancers tapped me on the shoulder and brought me on stage. We did the wave. The robot. I wormed. I spun, briefly, on my back. Paraparaumu Town Hall rocked that night, unlikely to have ever beheld such questionably rad acrobatics. I'd worn shiny ski-pants in preparation. I had on a headband and fingerless gloves.

It felt good being the centre of attention but generally I had to fight my tendency to want to overcompensate and appear fancier than I was: fresher, smarter, worldlier, more interesting. I often wanted to reinforce or explain my uniqueness, to double-down on a perception I thought already existed. Which made dating a bit weird. I sometimes wanted to adopt a louder, more intriguing persona. It took different forms. More cultured perhaps? Somehow removed from status games.

When social media became a thing I was shy of photos. On dates I'd want to stay away from beaches. Avoid the midday sun.

I could get paranoid. That Italian girlfriend who confides she has a thing for blonds and whose bookshelves are filled with the works of Oriana Fallaci, an impressive but also mildly fascistic journalist who once described Islam as a 'pool that never purifies'. The Iranian girl who calls you 'White Walker'. Half-jokingly. Half-resigned.

Twice I've been on dates where guys nearby have leaned in to chat to whomever I'm with.

'You with this guy?'

A slight guffaw.

For a moment that feeling of inadequacy passes through me. Timeless. Cold in my gut like ice-water. Like being told to go home or get back in your channel. Breathe. Relax. Laugh it off. Whoever really knows what it's about.

When I travelled, in the back of my mind I wondered whether how I looked would matter.

Visiting the Jewish Museum in Berlin, with its remembrances of the Holocaust, I look through the glass at photos of Hitler Youth. Apart from the uniform they just seem to be kids on camp. Everything I know about myself separates us. They're not me but they look like me. I notice someone looking in my direction. They turn to the photos then back to me again. They have an angry expression. I step away and head towards the exit.

Just by the door there's what looks like an old school arcade machine with a single load screen. It asks whether Mel Gibson's *The Passion of the Christ* is anti-semitic. Without any irony I can discern, it indicates the joystick and says MOVE LEFT FOR YES OR RIGHT FOR NO. I wobble it uncertainly, thinking it can't be serious, trying to understand why it's there after all that impactful and complex record of human history and division.

THANK YOU FOR YOUR ANSWER it says.

There's a zoo in the centre of Berlin. It's near the houseboat I'm staying on that's run by Captain Edgar, a Kiwi. I take the U-Bahn with its canary-yellow trains. They have schnitzel sandwiches and vanilla milk available at each stop. From the window I see two people stuck in the revolving door of an office building. Frustrated, they're both trying to appear polite and apologetic but also both refusing to let go or stop pushing. At the zoo I see a kea. The first time for me. Bright green. Curious and aggressive.

Beautiful but caged. The enclosure seems too small.

I walk by and there are ducks wandering about on the grass. A lady shouts at me in German, waving her hands. She's telling me, I think, to pass one over to her. I chase one for a minute before wondering what I'm doing and stop. I really have no idea what she's saying. I'm speaking English but she won't acknowledge it. I don't understand and she just keeps on yelling. I back away.

I catch up with Kiwis living in the Prenzlauer District. They're loving Berlin's cheap rent and liberal arts scene. I tell them I'd like to visit somewhere a bit warmer.

'You want to go to Spain or France? Oh you'll be fine. They love people like you.'

I assume I'll move through customs easily but I don't. In transit, bearded, with a backpack and a bit dishevelled, I stand out. They want to talk to me.

'You're travelling light.'

'What are you up to?'

And when I catch sight of myself in the mirror I don't feel safe. I feel singled out. I know it will show and my cheeks will go red. I won't be able to control it. I'm like the Incredible Hulk, but for embarrassment.

In Brazil some people call out.

'Hey, Allemagne!'

You're a type locals know. More familiar than a gringo. It's said without malice, with recognition and warmth. Here the multitudinous shades of skin colour are discussed in depth and celebrated, almost fetishised. I meet a guy whose nickname is 'Seis da Tarde'. 6pm. Not quite light, not quite dark.

I rent a motorbike. As I walk through the blazing heat to the rental stand the business owner sees me coming from a long way off. He's black, but also dark, almost purple.

'Ha,' he says. One hand upwards indicating the sun. 'You're very white.' Matter-of-factly. Smiling.

'You're very black,' I reply.

I shouldn't have said that, embarrassed for being simultaneously ungracious and foreign. Luckily he's caught the 'very' part and knows what I'm getting at. He pauses one second then laughs, shrugging his shoulders with some degree of shared acknowledgement.

Back in Wellington I bump into one friend then another, who both happen to be blond and pinkish like me. We haven't seen each other for a while and sit down at a café for coffee and a catch-up. Immediately the comments start.

'Ha! Look!'

'Like brothers!'

'Better watch out!'

Someone we don't know takes out a camera. It's an odd feeling. None of us like it so we pack up and leave.

The urge to locate yourself in relation to the world is natural. As a kid I used to get Santa Claus and God mixed up. I had the impression they were both bearded, magical caucasian men who lived far away. I wasn't allowed to see them directly, they did good things for me, and I likely owed them something I'd never really understand. A bit like my uncle who got me to breakdance at his wedding.

I wrote a postcard to Santa asking him for a pet. I wanted a dog but I was prepared to negotiate. I remember signing it:

New Zealand
Pacific Ocean
Southern Hemisphere
Planet Earth
The Milky Way

There's a strong argument that my childhood and my ethnicity are both privileges. In terms of almost every opportunity I can't disagree. There's a continuous messaging about the superiority of whiteness just below the culture's water-line. To assuage ethnic anxieties we often attempt to drown out their complexity with the absolutism of nationalism or chauvinism. Maybe I just have some nervous response to the hierarchy of colour that floats through our culture. Also to the bullish type that unquestioningly embraces these unspoken tribal borderlines. Puffed up. Declarative. 'Big buffalo', my girlfriend's mum calls them.

It's dying out apparently. Blondness. It's a recessive gene. Which might not be a bad thing considering the prominent blond pinkness of a couple of recently elected world leaders. Are they tapping into some resurgent ideology? Is it intentional? Discourse and rhetoric that once seemed so distant and remote is now suddenly close-up. Ideology traverses oceans, overflows from screens into homes. Personal. Nearby. Full of consequence.

One of the funny things about ageing is that a thing like pinkness seems to matter less and less. The currents and eddies of external and internal identity get so intermingled it's hard to tell which came first. The solipsistic navel-gazing. The introspection. Over such a superficial thing. Who has time for it? What you do for others is more important. So, you look like a policeman. Try not to wear too much blue.

I straddle something. But I don't know what. Not hybridised. Bicultural? Not really. Pākehā? Sure. I guess. I think being a touch different has just made me suspicious. I suspect my own idea of being woke, or anyone else that puts energy into making sure others see them as having arrived. I say this not because my pale shade gives me any view outside of whiteness but because I'm double-dipped. A bit alien as a result. A little aware of the theatre of identity since, it seems, I have more skin in the game.

'Our family could do with a touch more melanin,' my mum says.

Aunt Sally tells me the family genealogy. I'm a restless footnote struggling to stay awake.

I'm thinking of Abraham, washed from the stones. The crystal waves colliding. Not parting for him, but closing in. Their ineffable weight. That diaphanous web of white crests on the surface, constantly shifting. The light aqua of oxygenated water rolls alongside emerald-black depths that frighten me. Thalassophobia. The sense of ice-cold water and of losing your energy to the ocean. Dissipating. Of having fought waves to stay afloat only to lack the

power to swim to shore. Even though you can see it. The eerie calm of
knowing that. Seeing coastline after coastline. Fetlar. Hoy. The Out Skerries.
Zetland. New Zealand. Distance. Closeness. Geography. Opportunity.
Repetition.

Ko Pacific tōku moana.
Ko Tukituki tōku awa.
Ko Taranaki tōku maunga.

I shuffle my feet saying my pepeha. Even though the words are meant and
I'm proud of them. My tūrangawaewae.

Where you're born is like how you look. No one gets a choice about it. And
I'm used to doing a bit of a strange dance, identity-wise. A step forward, a
step back. Like Snagglepuss, I adjust my bow tie and fancy cuffs and try to
appear confident and articulate. To speak up. To say where I'm coming from.

I choose my words carefully. I know I'm more than one thing, like
everybody else.

Every potentiality doesn't have to be resolved. My emotions betray me now
and then. I do go red when I get things wrong, when my blood rises, but no
point being embarrassed about that now.

I'm glad it shows. At least that way you know I mean what I say.

Tender Gardens

[seventh lunar month]
小暑 *light summer* ⌒ *season of scorched hydrangeas*

> 'The Chinese were in fact very friendly, very nice to each other. Not what you'd expect.'

In the white-gold kitchen, the lights above the table are glinting. Pink and purple sweetpeas in a vase on the table flutter in a breeze from the open window. I feel my body become tense. I look out the window, because I can't look at anyone else. The heads of blue hydrangeas are swelling and pulsing in the manicured garden. Lily pads and lotus flowers tremble on the surface of the hot, brown pond. Dusk is beginning to fall.

Over breakfast I had been asking her about the flowers in her garden: hydrangea, peony, azalea, nasturtium. There are flowers I recognise but don't know the names of; she points to each one and tells me its name, giving me the vocabulary to write about plants for the first time. Azalea, clematis, dahlia, allium. She notices trees and flowers wherever she goes. Two years ago she visited Hong Kong—her first time. The city was so much greener than expected. So much green.

Her words are partly meant with good intentions, but I don't know how to carry them within my body. Does she think of my mother as *a Chinese*? Does she think of me as half *a Chinese*? If yes, how did she think I would respond? If not, then what am I to her? I ponder what I am doing here in this unusually cold northern-hemisphere summer.

When I was last at my parents' house I borrowed a book of theirs called *A Field Guide to the Birds of China.* On page 18, the beginning of a chapter titled 'The Avian Year', the rhythms of certain lines leapt out at me:

> China lies north of the equator ...
> And in the long days of the northern summer ...
> The birds are migrants descending in winter ...

According to an ancient Chinese agricultural calendar, each lunar month can be divided into two 节气—'solar terms'—and every solar term can be divided into three micro-seasons, each one characterised by a single event in the life-cycle of plants and animals. This means there are 72 small seasons within one lunar year. Every five days a new season comes.

When I first learned about the 72 seasons I obsessively translated and wrote down the most poetic ones I could find. I discovered that I was born during the month of lined clothing, in the solar term of summer's arrival, in the season of the untangling of deers' antlers. My mum was born during the month of gathering winds, the solar term of rainwater, and the season of wild geese flying north.

[twelfth lunar month]
夏至 *southern summer solstice* ～ *season of pōhutukawa flowers*

'If you spend too much time there, you might end up looking like this.'

The woman places one finger at the outer corner of each of her eyes and pulls. Cold breath leaves my body. I feel the urge to run to my dog, who is waiting for us in the back of the car, to hold his soft ears and press him close to my face. I resist this urge.

We've just come back from a walk on the beach and my dry lips taste like salt. The skin around my ankles is rough with sand and the hem of my dress is wet, heavy. We are almost within swimming distance of the great island that guards the shore. The island is a witness to what has occurred, is still occurring. The island is my witness.

It's January, midsummer on the Kāpiti Coast. In the northern hemisphere it's mid-winter, *the season of wild geese flying north*, almost my mum's birthday and almost lunar new year. It hasn't rained in more than a week and the edges of roses are beginning to scorch. Back in London, before we left, I planted spring bulbs (daffodil, iris, hyacinth) in plastic containers. I placed them in a line along the windowsill. I sent pictures of my not-yet-blooms to my mum, who replied to say she couldn't wait to grow some water hyacinths for this coming Chinese New Year.

[twelfth lunar month]
冬至 *deep winter* ～ *season of bulbs in the snow*

Is my otherness becoming more or less visible? Sometimes more—other mixed girls or women of colour approach me at work, kindly curious, wanting to know: 'You're mixed, aren't you?' Sometimes less—in a room full of white people they count me as one of their own, which makes me both invisible witness and invisible target.

Soon after moving to London, as the number of instances of casual racism I witnessed suddenly increased—both in London and when I went back to visit New Zealand—I began to realise the importance of keeping a record. I couldn't carry all the details in my body any longer; I needed somewhere to put them down, so I opened a new Google Doc and titled it 'INVISIBLE DOCUMENT'. I thought a spell of invisibility might help lessen the weight of it.

It was around this time that I also started to keep a garden diary. I became obsessed with gardens after seeing a kōwhai tree in a garden in north London. Its existence stunned me, all wrong at first, with no tūī diving towards its yellow bell-shaped blooms. Whenever I feel unsure of where I am and what on earth I'm doing so far from home, I think of the kōwhai tree. Where did it come from? Who planted it there? How many people, like me, have stopped in their tracks at the sight of it?

I found a purple crocus pressed between the pages of my copy of *A Cruelty Special to Our Species* by Emily Jungmin Yoon, a Canadian poet of Korean descent. I must have picked the flower in late winter and put it in the book for safekeeping. Its petals have turned translucent, rendering the poem 'Bell Theory' visible *through* the flower itself:

> How to say azalea. How to say forsythia.
> Say instead golden bells. Say I'm in ESL. In French class
> a boy whose last name is Kring called me belle.
> Called me by my Korean name, pronouncing it wrong.
> Called it loudly, called attention to my alien.[1]

The speaker of the poem begins accumulating half-rhymes, small chiming bells: *lie, lie, library, azalea, library*. I'm reminded of a line from a poem by British poet Rachael Allen: 'Women's bodies collect materials the way metals accrue in organs.'[2] I begin collecting the names of flora and fauna that sway in the background of my memories: azalea, magnolia, hydrangea, jasmine.

Since I am split between northern and summer hemispheres, my own 72 seasons are different. On my small sunlit balcony at the back of my flat in north London I begin planting a vegetable garden. I observe my little garden passing through various seasons: the season of sunflower seedlings, the season of wet jasmine, the season of cabbage butterflies alighting on broccoli leaves. But what does it mean to begin to put down roots in a country that forever finds you alien, an outsider, exotically mixed?

[first lunar month]
立春 the beginning of spring ⌒ season of glasshouse orchids

'On which side, your mother or your father?' He asks without preamble. The man, a friend of a friend I've met only once before, stands in the doorway of my blue kitchen. His body takes up the entire doorframe. He leans over me and I can see pores in the damp skin of his nose. He smiles down at me in a way that makes him look like he's baring his teeth.

Behind me, steam rises from the pot of boiling water where the jiaozi I made for our Chinese New Year dinner party are beginning to float to the surface, which means they're done. It's one of those cooking techniques I can't remember learning, only that my mum must have taught me at some point, just as she taught me how to put my forefinger in the pot of uncooked rice and pour in cold water up to the second knuckle. Steam coats the walls and my skin. I turn away from him to lift the jiaozi quickly from the pot and answer, 'On my mum's side.'

In late February we go to see the orchids at Kew. Up close they look more like animals than flowers. Pink mouths, violet tendrils, yellow tongues pressed up against the steamed-up glass. Their ancestors once grew wild in rainforests of Southeast Asia, like in Borneo, where my mum was born. There are curtains of climbing fluorescent blooms above a koi pond and a floating fibreglass Buddha surrounded by tea candles. I'm not sure if the display is meant to make me feel at home or if it's designed to make English people feel as if they've stepped into an exotic jungle. It can't be both.

When we exit the make-believe rainforest and re-enter wintry daylight, I see that the lake by the glasshouse is frozen over. Its fountain is encrusted in ice. In the giftshop I buy a dark purple orchid for £4 from the sale table, even though I know that means it's probably half dead.

9:57pm
do you have any orchid care tips?
what should I do once the flowers are drooping?

Mum 10:40pm
Prob means they are ready to drop!
Main thing is to resist repotting them.
Only a little water. Do not put in direct sunlight—
too hot; avoid windowsills. But still lots of light.

[first lunar month]
雨水 *rainwater* ⁓ *season of cold mandarins*

Who was the first New Zealand-Chinese writer? If one like me existed before the mid-twentieth century, their name has not been remembered. 'We had no artistic or literary role models,' poet and novelist Alison Wong writes in her essay on being a Chinese New Zealander, titled 'Pure Brightness'. Instead of reaching far back into history, I need only look around me.

Alison Wong writes of the sinking of the SS *Ventnor* off the coast of Hokianga in 1902. It was carrying the exhumed bones of 499 Chinese people back to China for reburial in their ancestral villages. Wong recounts a gathering in April 2013 to commemorate the sinking:

> We bow three times before apples, mandarins, almond biscuits, roast pork, baak jaam gai with feet and legs and head, red paper folded in the beak. We scatter rice tea wine; burn paper money gold; eat pork and baak jaam gai, an unwrapped sweet on the tongue. Electric fire crackers bang bang bang over the sand.[3]

How many hungry ghosts can the sea hold? Like Wong, I have these long-ago sea voyages as part of my ancestry. From Wales to Aotearoa on one side; from China to Malaysia to Aotearoa New Zealand on the other. When I ask my mum what we know about my grandmother's early life, I get a series of tentative facts. She was (*likely*) born near Hong Kong and fled war as a young girl with her family by boat to the Malayan Peninsula. Her father, my great-grandfather (*probably*) didn't make the boat or (*possibly*) died on the journey. Po Po's ashes were scattered in the sea off the coast of Kota Kinabalu last year.

Wong's poem 'The River Bears Our Name' contains two places that are in my bones. It is the first time I have encountered them together in a single poem and, as a result, I can feel this poem unfurling somewhere deep inside me as if it has always been there.

As the sun eases red over Pauatahanui
You stand alone at the Huangpu River
Layers of dust catch in our throat
The water is brown with years of misuse

You stand alone at the Huangpu River
Your card lies still open on the table beside me
The water is brown with years of misuse
I write out your name stroke upon stroke[4]

In moments of grief we offer up flowers, fruit, poems. Whenever we drove from the airport round the coast of Kota Kinabalu to my grandparents' house in Likas Bay, we would pass the great blue mosque and the Chinese cemeteries up in the hills, colourful gravestones cascading down the hillside. Some graves were draped in garlands of plastic chrysanthemums, with enamel bowls of mandarins, joss-sticks and folded paper money. Mum cleaned out Po Po's kitchen and gave me a box of her things: ivory chopsticks with 百年好合 engraved on the handles, melamine trays we bought for her from Daiso, enamel mixing bowls, and a dark blue enamel pot with a matching lid. I select the blue pot as a new home for my orchid from Kew Gardens.

[second lunar month]
惊蛰 the awakening of insects ～ season of first magnolias

'Lots of the Chinese girls at my school seem to be scared of dogs.'
    'That's because they eat them.'
    When the man seated across from me offers this response, a white-hot cloud of light billows up from the centre of the room, or from the centre of me. In the split-second after his words settle on my skin, I could choose to breathe or not breathe. I could speak or not speak. The plate on my lap holding a warm chocolate brownie tips forward. Melted vanilla ice-cream dribbles over onto the dark blue fabric of my skirt.
    'That was racist,' I say into the air, into the circle, my voice calm. For a moment my voice is present among the other voices and then it isn't any more. If anyone else in the room has heard, they don't make a sign. The room cannot hold on to the words for too long or else it might go up in flames. The room cannot hold on to me.

Over the course of the following day I feel sick and shaky. I have no appetite except for wanting to chew on something rich and soft, like a Cadbury caramel egg. I get up in the middle of the night and cut a blood orange, tearing the dark red flesh from the pith with my teeth. Outside, the wind stings my eyes and the first magnolia petals are starting to fly off the trees.

On my way home from work I buy a houseplant that opens its pink-veined leaves during the day and closes them at night, furling in on itself, making its limbs smaller in the dark. I learn that when plants do this it is called *nyctinasty*: a circadian rhythmic movement in response to the onset of darkness. The plant's light receptors in its skin, called phytochromes, cause the petals or foliage to curl inwards, asleep. Crocuses do this, as do lotuses, hibiscus, tulips and poppies. The exact reason for nyctinastic movement hasn't yet been determined, but it could be the plant's way of protecting itself from night-time predators, or to conserve energy, or both. I watch my plant closely. It is a *Calathea ornata*, native to Colombia and Venezuela, part of a family of plants called prayer plants because of the way the leaves and leaflets rise up at dusk.

My anger has nowhere to go, so it silently opens and closes inside me.

[second lunar month]
春分 *nearing the spring equinox* ∽ *season of birds flying homewards*

To find a new poetic lineage I need to draw a line diagonally across the Pacific Ocean, connecting my two parts of the world. I begin with a slim book I checked out from the library, *Women of the Red Plain: An anthology of contemporary Chinese women's poetry*, translated by Julia C. Lin. I flick through the poems looking for traces of the familiar. Mei Shaojiang, a poet from Shaanxi province, measures time in things cultivated from the earth:

> Days are garlic and wild scallions, still sprinkling loose dirt,
> Days are newly rolled up hemp ropes, still damp with water
>
> Days are a thirst-quenching blue plum, a paper-cut silhouette
> Of farmers bent with grain under fierce sun on hills' plains.[5]

In the days after the incident in the lamplit living room I became increasingly attentive to the needs and rhythms of my balcony garden. I set seedlings on my windowsill on a floral-patterned plastic tray, one that Mum gave me when we cleared out my grandma's kitchen after she died, and watched them obsessively. I measured time according to each centimetre of growth. I watched the petals of daffodils turn papery and transparent, like discarded butterfly chrysalises. I let them wilt and soften in their damp beds.

Flicking through *Women of the Red Plain*, I decide to create my own translation of part of a poem by Bing Xin, titled 'Paper Boats' ('纸船'). Bing Xin was born in 1900 in Fujian province, one region from which Hakka people originally come. I created this translation in order to get closer to Bing Xin and her distant dreamscape of mountains and sea. I also wanted to get closer to the Chinese language, which I've always carried with me but lost pieces of over the years. I wanted to make my own paper boat. I carefully unfold Bing Xin's paper boat, add my own translation to the many already in existence, then re-fold it and release it into the body of water that is closest to me now: the River Thames.

母亲，倘若你梦中看见一只很小的白船儿，
不要惊讶它无端入梦。
这是你至爱的女儿含着泪叠的 万水千山
求它载着她的爱和悲哀归去。

  Mum, if you see a little white boat in your dream
don't be startled
It is full of your daughter's tears
It travels across ten thousand waves
to carry her heart home to you

[*second lunar month*]
春分 *spring equinox* ～ *season of white lilies*

On the day of the Christchurch terrorist attacks, because I'm so far away and don't know what else to do, I cut the last two daffodils still alive and take them with me to place in front of New Zealand House in central London, where piles of flowers and cards and little flags have accumulated on either side of the glass doorway—small mountains of grief.

On my way to the vigil that evening I see flowers everywhere. A man on the train has a white iris poking out of the pocket of his jeans. I'm holding a bunch of purple sweetpeas that I bought at the flower stall near Embankment Station. As I often do when I'm on the train at rush hour, I think about what it would be like if something happened just then. All the petals would fly up into the air and stay there, suspended. I step off the train at Hyde Park underground station and nearly collide with a girl on the platform carrying an enormous bouquet of white lilies in her arms. I understand that if I follow her she'll lead me to where I need to go.

London commuters stare at us and our armfuls of leaves and flowers as we carve a sweet-scented path through the crowded station entrance, walking against the current of the city to join the others. We find them all standing huddled on the grass around more valleys of flowers, arms around each other, singing softly, cheeks lit by electric candles flickering in the loud night.

[*fourth lunar month*]
清明 *pure brightness* ～ *season of koru ferns*

My mum's seaside garden in Wellington is made up of plants inherited from the house's previous owners and plants added by her over the years. It's beautiful in a haphazard, patchwork sort of way, the product of several people's hopes and dreams layered on top of each other. We inherited a giant aloe facing the sea, its red tentacles rising towards the sun; an old pōhutukawa that's been chopped back too far; dark purple hydrangeas; a slender apple tree; an unruly and abundant feijoa; and a yellow kōwhai. By the gate, one or two spring onions burst forth from the earth every spring—we don't know how long ago they were planted there but we snip them with scissors to put in our soup noodles. There was a withering wisteria above the deck that couldn't withstand the gale, now replaced by a bougainvillea that occasionally spits mouthfuls of magenta blooms. On weekends she is on her knees in the wet grass, composting and potting up new succulents, collecting up fallen feijoas and lemons. While my dad is out walking the dog on the beach, my mum collects bags of shells from the shore, whole ones and fragments, and spreads them between her plants, creating a bed of seashells resembling the bottom of the seafloor transported into our garden.

I begin to have recurring dreams of a garden that partly resembles my parents' by the sea but contains plants from various landscapes I've called home: a giant yulan magnolia with creamy basketball-sized blooms, a fig tree, fluorescent pink peonies. In the dream I am standing in the doorway of a high-ceilinged house looking up at the terraced garden, where a tall rosemary bush with bright violet flowers grows in the centre. There are furred peaches hanging from low trees and big orange and black butterflies hovering above lilac-coloured hydrangeas, some with parts of their wings missing, as if they would turn to dust when touched. There is a kōwhai, a lemon tree, and a red aloe.

Kiri Piahana-Wong is a New Zealand poet of Ngāti Ranginui, Chinese and Pākehā ancestry. Her poem 'Day by Day' tracks a series of solitary moments spent in the kitchen and in the garden:

> (iii)
> At home, in the garden.
> My fingers cup the dirt,
> pull up weeds, weigh
> and scour. It is mid-
> afternoon.
>
> Early evening reading
> manuscripts. I reach
> through the pages,
> pluck out a koru fern.
> It needs water, it needs
> nurturing. That's why
> I am here.[6]

To garden is to care for, to feed, to tend: to offer up your own tenderness to the earth. Some days, in this other island country the furthest point from the island where I was born, this is why I am here.

Endnotes
1   Emily Jungmin Yoon, *A Cruelty Special to Our Species* (HarperCollins: New York, 2018)
2   Rachael Allen, *Kingdomland* (Faber & Faber: London, 2019)
3   Alison Wong, 'Pure Brightness', published in *The Griffith Review*
4   Alison Wong, 'The River Bears Our Name', published in *Jacket2*
5   *Women of the Red Plain: An anthology of contemporary Chinese women's poetry*, trans Julia C. Lin (Puffin, 1993)
6   *Tātai Whetū: Seven Māori women poets in translation*, eds Marea Rakuraku and Vana Manasiadis (Seraph Press: Wellington, 2017)

HELEN LEHNDORF

Johanna Tells Me to Make a Wish

OK.

So there are some chickens ...

(... but not bantams. Bantam eggs are too small and useless. You need two bantam eggs for every regular egg. Who wants to crack four eggs into cake batter when you could just crack two? Having said that, one duck egg equals two regular chicken eggs, so a single duck egg would be enough for a cake. I know this from my childhood, which might suggest that my childhood was all bucolic and duck-eggy, but I also learned how to make bullets, sharpen knives and how the only place in our yard where I couldn't hear my parents fighting was down behind the tin shed where the passionfruit vine was. The moss was springy there and the passionflowers so elaborate. Sometimes I would be sitting under the passionfruit vine for so long I'd need to pee, so I'd just pee right there, onto the moss ...)

So there are these chickens, scratching at the ground in dappled sunlight ...

(... dappled sunlight suggests a sense of peace, don't you think? Of ease? The sweet mood of Hopkins' 'Pied Beauty' and all that ...) Diffuse sunlight through trees ... Can anything bad happen in dappled sunlight?
  Of course it can, but not here, not today. Because the chickens would not be scratching around for worms if they were frightened. For instance, if a gun had just been fired, they would be hiding under the hydrangea bushes. You might say that the example of a gun is a bit Chekovian, melodramatic, and that the chickens could still scratch for worms in the dappled sunlight while a woman told a man she was going to move out, or while a different woman stood, watching the chickens, trying to process the news of a scary diagnosis, wondering how she might tell people and how much time off work she would need for the surgery. Chickens could continue to scratch around during those things, it's true. However, no one has cancer in this yard and no one is leaving. These are not the chickens of juxtaposition.)

The chickens are white.

(*They are the white that white creatures are in children's books, like the white rabbit in Alice in Wonderland, not the white that white creatures actually are, which is often quite manky and greyish, stained on the underside with poo or grass or general muck. C'mon, these are wish-chickens.*
These chickens are small-boned yet capable of carrying a lot of weight.)

I am sitting with the chickens.
I am sitting on the porch steps, watching them cluck around.

(*Let's say I have a cup of tea in my hands, because then I have a reason to be sitting there and a cup of tea suggests a moment of leisure, a break from toil. If I were just sitting there you might think I was lazy, that I could be pulling weeds or hanging out laundry. Or if you didn't think that, you might worry that these were the chickens of juxtaposition after all and I was sitting there in a dazed, processing-bad-news sort of way, and that I'd tricked you into relaxing about the chickens.*)

I have a cup of tea.
I am relaxed.
I am sitting, with a cup of tea, on my porch steps.

It is a sunny morning and so I've let the chickens out of their run for a scratch around. All I'm thinking about is how when they find a worm or a grub they just gobble it down and then immediately keep on looking. They don't look happy or pleased.

I'm thinking about how birds can't really show emotion on their faces at all.

My tea is grand and hot, and is hitting the spot nicely.

It is hot, strong tea and these are some sturdy, nuggety little chickens that I have, and the sun is dappled on their glowing, pure white backs.

(*Honestly, you can relax. There is no*
'Monster at the End of This Book'.

No one wants a single thing from you, or from me,
no one is in trouble; there is no 'storm's-a-coming, Pa!'

Trust the dappled light, trust how clean the chickens are.)

To sit on the back step in the dappled sun,
with good fresh tea and six white chickens to watch.

This is it, Johanna. This is my wish.

DAVID GEARY

Doctor and Patient Privilege

So much depends upon the white picket fence
covered in your blood, my brother
Dr William Carlos Williams depends
on his prescription pad to write his poems

in between patients, pus and swabs
he jots notes about the plums in the fridge
that he ate, that she was saving.
No one talks about his golf score since the D.I.V.O.R.C.E.

And it all depends on your point of view
whether Dr XXXXX was wasting my time
by getting out his guitar and singing me his songs
when he found out I was in showbiz

and wanted my opinion of his 'Extinction Blues'.
He invited me to The Temple Bar & Grill Open Mic Night
as his song snuck out under his surgery door
to the waiting room of impatients

thinking WTF!!! in Tongan, Samoan, Fijian ...
You name it, pick a Pacific island.
All I wanted was some drugs
and a diagnosis. He gave me so much more

I'm sure he had a concept album somewhere.
Later, many years later, I heard the stats say
that if your health professional talks to you up front
about something other than your ailment, your injury

then you have a better chance of a complete recovery.
It's the holistic approach—flakey shit, healing all of me.
I never went to The Temple—I wasn't sure if it was ethical
Ethics isn't that somewhere near Sussex?

He left his C90 mixtape in my mailbox
I bet you anything you like that Dr William Carlos Williams and
Dr Anton Chekhov never made that sort of house call.
And, sure, they're great writers but aren't you worried

that while you had blotchy skin in the game
their heads and hearts were elsewhere
and they mixed up the pen and the scalpel
and left a sponge or a clamp inside

when they closed up with higgledy-piggledy sutures?
Would that explain the nagging itch the dull ache?
Also, I chopped the head off the white rooster
so the wheelbarrow is redder and there's leftover soup.

CHRIS STEWART

Your Father Was Also Buried

your father was made
of the air it took

to breathe for your
suffocated mother

when she was left
with holes your father

filled them with earth
even with earth

some holes couldn't be filled
then your father was made

of the wind it took
to blow the earth off

your buried mother
in the ice he found water

to soothe her burns
then your father was

the fire it took
to warm her

Faute de Mieux

The date ends at the threshold between restaurant and footpath. It's early, no later than eight based on the height of the sun, which means their date ran shy of an hour. The food came out fast, almost as if the chefs could tell a bad match from the docket (chicken pad thai, mild; and tofu pad see yeuw, as hot as possible), and Ky hoovered it down, but the conversation was such a flat stretch of desert highway that she lost any sense of time passing. It could have been hours. It could have been twenty minutes. Their date could have broken time and sucked them back to the 1990s.

Earliness heartens her. It's Saturday night, she's downtown, and the buildings are shining. The beautiful young people are overdressed and excited. Tonight hasn't even begun for the sober girls tugging their dress hems or for the solo girls texting while walking. Life is happening for other people, and seeing this is the first step to believing that some day it might come back to her.

Patrick feels it too; asks, 'Should we try some wine?' She reads the subtext in his sleepy tone and dejected face: *Since neither of us has anyone to go home and cry to, we might as well salvage this evening. Should we try wine?* Just like that, her boring dinner companion transforms into a battle-weary comrade. He wants to compare divorce scars over a few drinks, maybe even run a post-mortem on their date and wonder over the existential quality of their disappointment, how after a certain age, every bad conversation is a nudge towards the conclusion that there is no one, no one, no one out there.

'Yes,' she says. 'I'd like that very much.'

He's easier now that he's not trying to impress. They talk about the weird effect of walking past bars broadcasting different songs. She plays a game where she identifies the target demographic based on the music. Self-conscious uni students saddled with guiding their pack somewhere cool where they can drink cheaply and dance; straight men aged 40–50 who only go to bars to watch rugby; baby-boomers looking for somewhere to feel hip but where the music's not too loud. Patrick laughs and argues that people don't exclusively listen to songs written during the decade they were a teenager.

'Maybe on weekdays people listen to other music.' She's very good at talking, and it's sometimes quite a funny effect to let her mouth outrun her mind. 'But on a Saturday night? Out on the town? It's not about music or taste any more, right? It's about neon-lit, boozy capitalism. It's about these bars not being able to sell you the present tense with a straight face so they put these siren songs into a playlist and point their speakers towards the footpath to lure in passing sailors with the promise that through these doors, for the price of a drink, your youth is waiting to be reclaimed.'

'What?' Patrick says, laughing. 'Are you a communist or something?'

'What?'

'I don't know. You're on about capitalism.'

'Nah, I reckon I'm on about the intersection of time and money and human ego. Sort of transcends ideology.'

'What?' He's still laughing. 'You're a very weird woman.'

This date was set up by a friend, one of Ky's oldest, a high-school mate. They hadn't seen each other for fifteen years, and Ky felt special thinking that she had made a lasting enough impression for said friend to take a stab at a match. She feels less special now that she suspects her friend's idea of a match is just two single people.

The hope was that the set-up would offer a head start, get a few preliminary steps out of the way. Dating changed while Ky was married, accruing apps and shifting norms, and she doesn't understand ghosting or when to use the eggplant emoji. Trying to learn is exhausting, and it makes her feel like maybe this is futile. If she has to start from zero and get to the part where they're home from the afterparty of a cousin's wedding and making scrambled eggs at 2am, and they're gossiping, laughing and twirling on the kitchen lino so much that, gun to her head, she wouldn't be able to say which of them had buttered the pan or whisked the eggs or cracked the pepper, but the eggs come out soft and creamy, exactly how they both like them, well, she's not sure there's enough time left in her life to get from zero back to that.

'We're here,' Patrick says. They're at a nondescript door beside a dark-windowed accountant's office. He's punching a code into a keypad.

'Is this a speakeasy or something?' she asks, starting the question before she understands that this is an apartment building. She has just gone home with him.

'A what?' he laughs. He's been laughing like this the whole walk.

The fault was hers for injecting too much wishful thinking into his verb. *Should we try some wine?* Try, as in make a real, honest attempt to do something right. What he meant was try, as in the way everybody means it when they're talking about wine. Sip by sip. Also, now that she's thinking about it, he talked a lot at dinner about the wine club he joined to make friends post-divorce, and all the nice bottles piling up in his kitchen, since he has not made any friends and has no one to drink them with.

'This is actually a historic building,' he says, leading her down a carpeted corridor that reminds her of *The Shining*.

'Really?' she asks. It's freezing in the corridor and she tries to rub down the goosepimples on her arms. 'What happened here?'

'Nothing special, I don't think. It was a dry goods warehouse.'

He means historical, as in old. Not to be confused with historic, which would be important in history. If they were at a bar or restaurant, she might have explained this to him. There was no feeling she liked better than the discovery of something she didn't even know she didn't know, but she'd once corrected a guy for using 'infer' when he meant 'imply' and he straight up called her a cunt and walked off. You just never know how someone will respond. She does know, however, not to try to find out when they're alone in a dark corridor.

'I was a bit reluctant to buy this place, to be honest,' Patrick says as they wait for the lift. He keeps talking once they're in it. 'I mean, it's a great location but it seemed quite expensive for an apartment and I don't really need a place with two bedrooms, but then I figured, just go for it, right? If I don't end up staying here, I can find tenants. Not that the rental income would be a big money maker, but it's all about the capital gains in the end, and I reckon I'll have quite a bit of equity in thirty years. I've only been here a year and the value's already gone up 50k.'

She wonders if he's worried and that's why he's talking so much. He's taking quite a risk, bringing a stranger back to his place. She's smaller than him but she has a sizeable purse that could easily contain a knife or a revolver or a lead pipe or a candlestick.

'And voilà,' Patrick says, unlocking his door and swinging it open. It looks like a hotel room, all beige tones and chunky matching furniture. One wall has built-in bookcases, empty save six books, and the other walls are even emptier. It astounds her that a human could live in this space for more than a few days without going mad and tacking up a road map or a beach towel or literally anything.

'Red or white?' he asks, and for a second she thinks he's asking for advice on an accent colour, but then sees that he's veered into a tiled kitchenette. She'd forgotten all about the wine.

'Either,' she says, and drops her bag onto the arm of the sofa. She moves towards the bookshelf, with the intention of judging him by their covers, but her attention is caught on the way by three small taxidermised bats dangling from fishing line in the window-frame. This seems like a clear-cut case of her mind rendering something weird over the top of something normal, but when she gets closer to look, that's exactly what they are. Dead bats.

They're the size of mice, with leathery wings held tight around themselves, the posture of self-conscious girls. Their vacant eye sockets are patched over with grey felt, like heavy lids protecting a deep sleep. They have foxy little faces, which surprises her. She was expecting something stubby and creviced like a movie monster. Not these elegant snouts and delicate needles of teeth. Their ears are sail-shaped and velvety and thin enough to absorb the light coming through the window, taking on a warm, orange luminescence. She wants to touch one, to hold it in her hand and warm it back to life.

She doesn't like dead things and can't understand why someone would use them to decorate. But then again, neither would she ever consider finding someone to pay off her mortgage while equity accumulates. She's just not that into winning, and she's read enough Hemingway to know that winning is exactly why men collect dead animals.

'Do they scare you?' Patrick asks, seeming amused by the thought. He comes up beside her and hands her a glass of red wine.

'I've been living in Queensland,' she reminds him, happy to have reason for the words to crawl through her mouth. She's only been away from Cairns for a month and already she finds herself doing wistful Google Image searches on the city. Leaving was a necessity: she would never be able to do anything—not go to the petrol station, not to the dentist, not to check the mail—without potentially running into her husband and his twenty-two-year-old girlfriend and their fat baby. She went from, which is not to be confused with coming to. Wellington, city of her childhood, was *faute de mieux*, as in French for lacking anything better. 'I'm quite used to bats.'

'Big ones, I bet,' he says, with a tone that makes her think he's meaning to be lascivious. He sits beside her, with just a handspan of beige sofa between them.

'So what ...' She's careful to phrase her question in a way that won't allow the bats to stand as a metaphor for his dick. 'What made you decide on taxidermy and not, like, a poster or something?'

'I saw them in a shop.' He's looking at the bats, not at her, and she takes the opportunity to shift further down the couch. 'It was years ago, and I thought they were cool, but Penny, my ex-wife, wife at the time, thought they were creepy. So after we separated, I found some online and ordered them. Because I can buy whatever I want now.'

'Interesting.' She was right, they're trophies.

'What do you think?' He turns to her with a new intensity and she can't bring herself to make eye contact. 'Are they cool or creepy?'

She shrugs. 'They're cute up close. But in general, I'm going to side with your ex-wife. I'm just a bit averse to *memento moris*. Or *mementos mori*? I guess I've never seen the plural form.'

He shakes his head. 'What's that?'

'It's an object that reminds you of death.'

'That's a bit dark, to be honest. That they remind you of death. Most people say they remind them of vampires.'

'I guess I'm not most people.' This sounds flirtier than she intends it, as if she's challenging him to find her extraordinary. What she means is to offer him a way out: *I know I'm a very weird woman, we can just agree on this and go our merry ways.*

'I can tell you're a bit different,' he says, and she makes a face. 'I don't mean in a bad way! I think it's cool. It's like you're not trying to impress anyone, so I don't feel like I have to impress you. It's been ages since I've found it so easy to talk to a woman.'

She's fascinated by this concept of trying to impress. When she meets someone new, she offers a version of herself akin to practice scales, knowing as she does that the full opera can be a bit much for people who don't know what they've bought a ticket to. How funny to find a person with the opposite problem. A beige-wall guy with a fear of being a bit lacking. For the first time she feels a kinship with Patrick.

'To be honest,' he continues, 'it's been ages since I've been this comfortable talking to anyone. I had a lot of trouble opening up after the divorce.'

'Yeah, I get that,' Ky says. 'I moved to a different country to get away from it.'

'It wasn't just getting away from it. Penny was saying all these quite nasty things when we were breaking up. She really got into my head.'

'Like what?'

'Like that I'm passive, that I'm boring. That I don't have any ideas of my own.'

'Wow.' The kinship evaporates and she wishes they were in a bar or a park or a frozen yogurt shop, somewhere they could have a conversation. Alone in his lounge there are consequences, which means it's a job. She has to pick up his baggage, handle it without breaking anything, put it where he wants it and smile the whole time.

'So, for the first year after we separated, every time I talked to anyone, even just small-talk at work, the conversation would echo around in my head, but like it was being told back to me by Penny. It would just be hours of a voice telling me how I was weird and awkward and how I make people uncomfortable.'

'That's awful,' she says flatly.

'Yeah. It's getting better but it's still there, to be honest. I actually almost cancelled tonight. I'm glad I didn't.'

His hand slides onto her knee and what will happen next feels both inevitable and preventable. She doesn't care all that much about whom she has sex with, but he's clearly the type to care, and he'll make her breakfast in the morning, which means she'll owe him an explanation before exiting his life. The explanation would be painful, because a good, kind person would never have had sex with *faute de mieux*, so she will avoid that admission.

Instead, she will go on another date with him, then another. It will go on like this, lingering and languishing, until it ends one day for no particular reason.

It might be more ethical to stand up and walk away now, wander down the street until she gets sucked into a bar playing 'Torn' by Natalie Imbruglia and where at least one of the mixed drinks is named for an esoteric *Simpsons* reference. She'll play on her phone and poke at the ice in a gin and tonic until some guy exactly her age who's in town for business, and who definitely has a girlfriend back in Palmerston North or wherever, buys her a drink. She'll accept but will weasel out of following him back to his hotel room. Then she'll leave the bar and be out among the beautiful young people puking their KFC onto hundred-year-old buildings and limping off to damp flats with blisters biting their heels.

Patrick's hand is warm and heavy. He leans back against the sofa, relaxing, and his hand drags along her thigh like he's got no choice in the matter. His hand is attached to his arm, after all, which is attached to his shoulder, which just so happens to be going this way. The hand's journey ends at the threshold between out-in-the-open skin and under her skirt. Between plausible deniability and intent. His casual demeanour is so funny to her, and she swallows a sharp laugh. He thinks it's a hiccup and offers her a glass of water, which she turns down. She's fine, she tells him, it's nothing, and she leans over and kisses him.

JENNY POWELL

Meeting Rita*

Hanging around in the gallery
for a ticket-only discussion of fashion
we were singles leaning on opposite walls.

Judgement flicked like a whip
and we couldn't change a thing.
Rita and I were wearing the same coat.

Colour of deer in tussock terrain we
thought we were camouflaged
in high-country cover.

Corrugations of hills folded into our sleeves,
tumbled to the flat plains of cuffs.
Coat skin stripped of scrub,

border protection between out and in.

We sat together.

*Rita Angus (1908–1970)

The Poisson Effect

After a statistical analysis
our diagnosis was Poisson Distribution.
We had caught a pattern of never-
or-rare events, a random infection without
contagion yet we were kept in isolation.

How can we have it if it hasn't happened,
like an escalator up Mt Everest or streetlights
of solar-powered starfish?

Take the number of deaths by horse kick
in the Prussian Army, 1875 to 1894.
Chance events, just as improbable as the meeting
of Rita and me, but slightly possible.

There are no underlying systemic problems,
no likelihood of a scattering plot of surprising
coincidence.

It's just us.

Two women who were wearing the same coat.

Not All Colours Are Beautiful

There was nothing to say.
No Instagram instant, Facebook face, or snap to chat about.
Nor was there a 'happy to announce' in the daily times
or evening press or morning herald.

Nothing to report but two crises of identity; not-babies
instead of the real thing. Knot babies untied.
Their tiny anchors cast off too soon, unfinished bodies
awash in a sea of blood the colour of amaranth.

Amaranth

amaranth red. Colour of the dead.

How foolish words can be with their sticky webs,
their traps of history and botany that never leave.

Amaranth

grown in the garden of Greek gods it's the flower
that never fades. Everlasting. Immortal.

Amaranth dough mixed with beheaded blood
was baked for Aztec ceremonies.

Amaranth and honey, skull-shaped dessert
shared on Mexican Days of the Dead.

Hopi Indian red dye, Cherokee medicine
for menstruation, African porridge, Indian vegetable,
Vietnamese soup, Jamaican side dish,

and now,
'Crop of the future' as if it were a recent discovery.
Gluten free, complete protein, cholesterol lowering, packed
with iron and Vitamin C.

I am wrong, Rita. I am sorry.
There is always something being announced
and love, love that nearly was but wasn't,
that kind of love never fades.

The Story about the Wooden Boy

Not another chapter in this story about the wooden boy, they thought as they lay on either side of the marriage bed, too afraid of rupture should they touch. Was it them? Had they chosen the wrong timber to create him? Was there something lacking in *his* stubborn grain or *her* head-in-the-clouds heart that had fashioned him askew? Or had it been in their shaping as he grew? Were their hands not as gentle as they could have been? Had their chipping-away been too rough? Had the day-to-day rub of competing with a brighter, more troubled sibling worn him in the wrong places, or was it the failing of others not to choose him for the school team, or the house falling down in the middle of the night? Had their attention wandered to different projects that seemed more important at the time—painting a room, writing a new line, their *sorry-son-not-nows*? What inner voice had made him listen to the fox on the corner yipping on about an easy fortune? Should they have kept him inside? Had they not given him a Jiminy Cricket in a box when he was seven? Why his need to play with donkeys who wore gold chains around their necks and popped pastel beans and drank rivers of consumerist rap nonstop? How had he come to be sleeping on Suffolk Street in an abandoned car, owing money, wearing unwashed clothes, and dealing with crooks? How had they come to be on this broken raft inside these ribs of sadness, wishing hard for blue flashing lights to surround him, so that a real boy may return and save them?

RACHEL O'NEILL

The Place of the Travelling Face

When I peer outside all I see is darkness and a reflection of shoulders with nothing above them. Earlier the bulb in the lounge blew. We became a family of voices, hard to distinguish from the family on the radio. But a boy whispered to his beloved horse and then he got his pistol out and shot it. My grandmother explained that life is a great mystery and then that mystery ends. I continue to stare out the window and, as I touch around the place of my travelling face, I wonder.

Escher

I get motion sick. I have since I was a small child. I also get nauseated by stasis, shellfish, and having the same haircut for more than three months. For a really long time I was sick in a way that felt more like scrambling. That moment when you're almost asleep and the world drops out from under you, but without shift, for over a decade, without even a satisfying crunch.

I'm not any more. I'm the happiest I've ever been in my life. I am still so sad, so much of the time. I mostly try to make other people laugh.

Nothing leads where I thought it would. I wasn't told about all the new things that would start hurting. I'm going to see my parents die. I might see my little brother die. That never used to be true.

Is recovery just moving from one set of fears to another, equally towering? Now that I kind of want to live, all I can do is imagine things I'm not sure I could live through. I have a real good imagination.

The world is so hopelessly big, with an enormity of grief that I cannot fix. Mistakes made before I was born that I can't undo.

When I pray, I pray for God to crush me. I want to start over, and over, and over and over and over and always be bathed in novelty and never ever grow around things again. In standing still you open yourself to being seized by loss.

When I was sixteen I was in love with a girl. She always wore the same perfume, and I still have a bottle of it in my desk. I last saw her on 17 February 2012. I was rubbing her back as she threw up into a bucket in my bedroom. I didn't write a poem that wasn't about her for five years, and I wrote a lot of poems. It's now been eight years and I'm coming to the conclusion that she will never become someone I haven't met. The world is so hopelessly big, and imperfectible. Some of the mistakes are mine and I can't do anything about those ones either.

This doesn't feel like coming home and it doesn't feel like building a home and it still, a quarter of a century in, does not feel like I belong here. It just feels expanded. I have more space than ever to feel disconnected from.

When I write in my journal about the psych ward I call it 'Antarctica'. Perhaps it's fitting that Antarctica is disappearing from the poles as fast as it's disappearing from my head—perhaps that makes me God? When I pray, I pray for God to crush me and it never comes. I never lift my hand. I lie awake at night, fantasising about the two point four metres it would take. I want to sleep. I am tired. I am so tired.

Right now, there is a concrete wall being built through the middle of the National Butterfly Centre in Texas, and it is going to cause the extinction of dozens of species within the next few years. That is not something a person would do, that is something from a story, and yet it's *happening* and there is nothing I can do about it. When I found out I sent them all the money that was in my account that week—fifteen dollars—and then spent a long time trying to decide why I felt even guiltier.

I'm so tired. I haven't made it to Jerusalem yet. I'm sorry, Hemi, I will get to you, it's just that I still have too many days I can't peel myself off the bottom of a bottle.

If 2017 was the hospital year, 2018 was the year I watched someone I love receive so many death threats she couldn't leave the house. Eventually she moved to China, where no one knows her name. A year of finding community at last, at last, and then realising there's actually no room for people like me, and then the same, again and again, and I feel like maybe all the people like me died in the 80s? I can't speak to the plague, but I also can't speak to the warmth of a patchwork quilt.

I am tired. Now that I've finally stopped dissolving, everything is dissolving around me. Every time you turn your back, something disintegrates and returns almost the same but slightly worse. Diseases that used to be gone aren't gone any more. Countries falling into the sea. I don't have a single friend who doesn't have panic attacks. The world is becoming something else. Tell me you can feel it. I should be writing. I should be working, I should be making gifts for my friends or sewing toys for my nephews or writing my—
When was the last time you felt like there was nothing and nowhere else you should be?

We've come so far—I have so much unshakeable faith, and I think it might be killing me, I think it might be what's always been killing me—was it all just to get here? Is this it? We are the only species to have ever buried their dead with flowers, and we can't do anything now that the world is drowning? How can that possibly make sense? It doesn't, but that's what's happening, so what am I supposed to do? I finally plan to live past twenty-five.

I am sick of always ending these poems with fear.

Already

You won't remember this
this pummelling whoosh
a late slowing train
shunting all notions
purposes aside,
the clapping
cloudburst.

In this struggling
season where tūī
flash from flax to flax
shedding dead crickets
monarchs quiver
in frail draughts
bees stop-go lawn order
ruthless runners
middle-finger gravity
orange fizzles
and crimson drifts fringe
heat-weeping streets
we meander about our undoings

in sleepy bays aliens
cupping phones like compasses
haunt shadows
gleeing kids break waves
till icecream mokos.
These days are giant.

Another year and you
you need me less
your shoes are small
again, your hair is longer,
and I slow and sway softly
from the sidelines.

BOB ORR

A Whaleboat in Kororāreka

Walking back from a jetty of charter boats
I'm caught by a thunderstorm
and duck into a lean-to abutting the museum.
Above a whaleboat in Kororāreka
a security camera's lens
panoramic as a whale's vision
observes me without blinking.
From the gunnel to the bilge
I stroke lines curved sweet as latitudes.
There is daylight between the strakes—
in the evening there will be stars.
To be flooded thus and perhaps to founder
might be the only way to comprehend the whale of actuality.

Once a cedar in North America where Indian spirits
flew with the wind
you shape-shifted on a shipwright's floor
sawdust and shavings mingling with salt air—
sea-kindly your hull from stem to stern was fastened.
Decades later you fetched up on this coast
discovered first by Kupe funnelling the future
from Hawaiki across Moana-nui-a-Kiwa to Aotearoa.
And afterwards came Cook tacking to and fro
like an albatross before sailing off.

You knew headlands like whales—
on certain days you heard them singing.
Offshore by black rocks at low tide basking
over sandbars and estuaries half-mooned with mysteries

your steering oar tilted to
the sea-rippled stingray-shadowed shark-disturbed sand.
You knew wave slap and musket crack
ships' biscuits and breadfruit
waiata and sea shanty
reveries and revelry.

From Busby to Brash
both of them like gannets shitting in mid-flight
you've seen the crap come down.
I think of an urupā hemmed with gorse
where giant kauri barnacled and bulky
as their cousin the cetacean once stood tall.
I look out across the bay
to the Treaty Grounds—
its anchor stone preventing Aotearoa from being swept away.
By a whaleboat in Kororāreka
I dream of a blue continent where the spermaceti whale's balm
leaves in its wake a road of ineffable calm.

Magic Hour

'Morning shift again, baby?'

Anya gave a look while she exhaled smoke out the window, the sun about to reflect over the lake. She was in her good red panties and a dirty pale singlet. She hugged her knees; already the rising sun outlined her face. 'Just got in. You missed a good party.'

Linnet shrugged. She didn't like Anya's boyfriend and his scrap-filled parties with crushed can after crushed can next to the propane tank, his drunk loudness, like he owned the place, no visa problems. Pāua shells filled with wet cigarette butts and clumpy ash. Sticky-brown pipes and bongs knocked off the outdoor table. When he got going he'd make all the girls call him 'Captain'. Like they weren't all in the same shithole in paradise. Even though Linnet had been living with Anya in their tiny two-room cabin for almost a year, she still felt shy about asking her for a ride if Anya wasn't going in to work too. The hotel wasn't far per se, past the centre of town and a kilometre's walk up a hill, but the buses were infrequent and expensive.

'Bye, baby.' Anya's eyes were glazed. She'd been smoking.

There was a theme-park-like, old western goldminer's history to the town and the wealthy tourist present: big hotels and empty holiday mansions. And there was nature, there was always nature, the lake and the mountains still beautiful, even to Linnet, that morning.

The cabins that had once been a campground ('the Smith') had since been repurposed as the only affordable housing for hospo workers—seasonal, migrant workers; the people who scrubbed the toilets in the big hotels and waited for the first delivery of the morning at Shotty's 7-Eleven. The grounds were on a ridge, smack behind one of the biggest, richest hotels in town, right on the Esplanade. Esplanade used to mean the wide, flat strip around a city's fortress walls, exposing enemies or anyone who lived beyond—the feudal poor, the villagers. It was about access. By the time of the Victorians, the word esplanade was synonymous with seaside resorts. Esplanades allowed the wealthy to be seen, no matter the state of the tide. Their shoes kept dry and clean.

The developers must have thought the guests would never look behind them, past the delicate landscaping, strategically placed pool-houses and other anonymous utility structures. They would always be looking forwards at the lake and mountains, or lovingly at their new wife or lover, or tipping the room service, but never looking backwards at the Smith. It was funny that Linnet and Anya's cabin looked out at the same thing—the shock of blue lake and snow-capped peaks. They had the same view as the holidaying super-rich. Even though they see us they cannot see us, Linnet thought.

She set off down the hill to cut through town. In the early morning the Smith still felt like a campground, the sense of permanence and boredom not upon it yet. As if the children were still asleep. Because what is a campground without kids? The slipshod pale yellow, pale green or pale purple tiny two-room cabins sans property lines, maybe a clothesline or a dented barbecue in between. No tall black fence or carefully sculpted lavender, flax or toetoe demarcating what large swathe one owns from the one someone else owns.

Most of the cabins had two rooms and a semi-detached bathroom. A room to eat in, a room to sleep in, and a room to shit in. Rent was $450 a week and the cabins were freezing. Last week at a party Anya's boyfriend rambled on about a developer finally taking over the Smith. This had been the talk for as long as Linnet had lived there. Anya's boyfriend had been at the Smith the longest, and he was Australian, which meant he could leave and go home whenever he wanted, not needing a visa, just a plane ticket away. Linnet thought about how much power it gave him, to move freely between this country's borders and his own. She wondered if New Zealanders thought about that too. She hated the way he'd give drugs to Anya for a smile, for a kiss. Most of the tenants had landlords they'd never met or were crashing. The seasons not changing but blurring into the next. Sometimes people talked about where they were from, but Linnet didn't.

On Main Street the tour offices were stirring, cafés opening, outdoor wear and gift shops readying. Linnet's favourite place was the office of the *Otago Daily Times*. She would sit outside in the coffee shop next door and spy on the whiteboard, names in a grid next to codes for stories she didn't understand. Surfaces covered by newspapers, the odd person walking into another room with a mug in his hand. She imagined herself in that office, covering a *beat*, but she hadn't been to university, her daydreaming was based on movies like *All the President's Men* and *Flight of the Condor*, or she'd be a journalist like Hunter S. Thompson in California. Califor-ni-a. Cali. So-Cal.

She bought a paper at the stand. It was the 'year in review' edition, and on the cover was a story about a thirty-five-year-old National MP who'd bought a second townhouse for almost a million dollars. Newsworthy. In the photograph his features were handsome: his dull blue eyes, tanned skin, sandy blond hair and straight, chemically whitened teeth made him look like an American quarterback posing for his college photo. He dripped wealth. He was a 'good bloke' who described himself as working hard. She set the paper down. A bleached-blonde woman in a tight floral top walked out of the office with a small girl, then crouched down to help the girl blow bubbles out of a bottle clutched in her chubby hand. Linnet stiffened, worried that she'd been caught staring at the office window. Was she allowed to be out here on the street? The bubbles floated in Linnet's direction and the woman said, 'Now let's watch out for this pretty lady.' Linnet didn't know how to respond to this, so she didn't. The nice words so offhand. In spite of herself, Linnet's eyes teared up behind her sunglasses for a moment as the glossy bubbles suspended themselves around her, beautifully still.

Soon the sidewalks would be crowded and the streets gridlocked with rental cars and tour buses, the one street through town a bottleneck.

Cresting the hill, the lake to her left, she looked at the ground to shade her eyes. She didn't have her work shirt on yet because she knew how sweaty she'd be by the time she clocked in. She hated that they wore all black when it was so hot, but white uniforms showed stains easily. Today was going to be a bad day. It was New Year's Eve. It was going to be bad because tomorrow would be worse. She would clean everything today, knowing the wasted mess of the tourists on New Year's Eve would await her on New Year's Day, a day that would mark the longest time she had worked without a day off. Eighteen days, but she needed the money.

She walked in the back entrance to the staffroom and pulled on her shirt, stuffed her backpack in the locker. Her manager, who went by the name Jez, appeared with three girls behind him. Jez had once explained how girls were best for cleaning—especially Asian girls, whom guests noticed less. He would say this with a wink at her and Linnet would imagine stabbing him with one of the hotel's cheese knives, and then she would be frightened by the violence of this fantasy. She was always afraid men could tell when she had bad thoughts. That's why they had all the good jobs.

'Some newbies today, and you're showing them the ropes!' Jez said with exaggerated deference. Linnet was showing them the ropes because he would leave by midday, already sipping from his flask and making loud phone calls to his mates about the evening's plans. When he came back from a trip to Thailand he had bought all the girls oversized T-shirts with a female stick figure on all fours sucking a stick figure's dick and being fucked in the arse by another stick figure. Jez slapped his hands together loudly and walked away.

Six hours later Linnet and the three girls were still making the rounds. They worked mostly in silence and didn't ask any questions, just did what she did or followed her instructions. They were in the home stretch of the shift in an easy, comfortable rhythm by mid-afternoon. Linnet had her headphones on listening to her simulated rain app, completely in the zone, when she opened the door to room 33. Normally she would have propped the door open with the cleaning cart and opened the door to the opposite room for two of the other girls to clean, but she stopped dead as she walked in. The room smelled strongly of piss, rotten food, synthetic materials and sweat. She had a sharp taste in the back of her throat like she'd just done a bump of coke. There were about a dozen used condoms on the plush carpet, and the smell reminded her of the smell of her fingers after she wore rubber gloves to wash the dishes at home. She took out her earbuds. The other girls entered the room. Linnet heard gasps.

'Fuck this shit,' said the girl with light brown hair and a heart-shaped face, whom Linnet would have sworn was European but was now obviously, matter-of-factly, American.

'That is shit on the wall, for real.'

Linnet was self-conscious, flustered. She had thought their silence was an easy acceptance that they couldn't understand each other. The two other girls looked at her.

'I mean you gonna call Biohazard or what? I'm not going in that bathroom.' The girl started to walk around the room. She opened the sliding glass door to the balcony.

'My manager left for the day,' Linnet said finally.

The girl was on the balcony now, breathing deep. She turned around and looked back at Linnet, the blue of the lake and the tall mountains outlining her. Linnet wasn't used to this, the ease with which the girl leaned on the rail looking back at her through the wide doorway. Linnet wasn't used to being looked at. The girl walked back into the room and went to the bedside table, picking up a man's gaudy, expensive watch.

'Hey,' Linnet said, 'we're almost done here. This is one of the last rooms.' Where had the other girls gone? Suddenly they weren't there. They, at least, would still have their jobs and visas tomorrow.

'You fucking serious?'

Linnet had lived as a non-citizen as long as she could remember, watching even the slightest infringement of the rules with near panic. Who was going to pay for this? The American put the watch in her back pocket, went to the mini-fridge and grabbed a bottle of the most expensive champagne and a bottle of Haitian rum, then threw on a lush camel hat that was on the table, grabbed some cash out of the bureau, and walked out of the room. As if possessed, Linnet was following her down the hallway. They walked fast, then ran down the stairs into the staffroom. The girl shoved the bottles into her backpack, which Linnet grabbed before following the girl's average height out into the light of the last day of the year.

'You need a ride?'

They sat at the lookout with the van parked behind them, the tall grass itching their dangling legs. Technically, it wasn't Rey's van, she was just borrowing it from a friend. Rey was from Pennsylvania, and when Linnet said she didn't really know what Pennsylvania looked like, Rey said it looked a lot like here, spreading her arms wide. After the hotel, Rey had driven off like a madwoman, laughing, and Linnet started calculating when the crime would be reported.

'Oh please, some cash and booze on New Year's Eve? Blame it on me.'

They had picked up some sandwiches and driven up to a lookout Rey said no one would know about. There would be fireworks at midnight. As they ate and talked and passed the rum back and forth, saving the bubbles for the witching hour, Linnet couldn't remember the last time she felt this good.

Linnet asked Rey how long she'd been here.

'Leaving soon—you gotta get out of here every three months, they say. Something about the vibrations in the mountains and the mineral content of rocks and such. If you don't leave you start to get crazy, feel depressed. Have you ever seen people have sex in hotels? Sex in hotels is always nasty.'

'I haven't seen them, but I've heard them.'

Rey was just passing through on her way to whatever came next. Rey was short for Reyna, and she knew a lot about gold and movies. That's why she wanted to come here. They had gold here, and they film movies. In Pennsylvania they had a bit of gold, but oil was bigger. The town she was from, in western PA, was full of rust, had a shitty mining museum, a bank, an American union, a Perkin's Diner, her grandparents, and a lot of meth. That was it. When she talked it was in long bursts, as if she wasn't used to being interrupted, but she asked a lot of questions too.

Linnet wouldn't answer all of the questions. When Rey asked her what she was doing here, Linnet knew for the first time that she no longer remembered. Where was Linnet from? It no longer seemed to matter. She worked, but it would never be enough. She lived but it was no living, just a routine, never enough money to get out, or time enough to figure something else out. She had almost forgotten what brought her here in the first place—a boy she liked had invited her down to work on a ski resort for the season. She remembers showing up at the resort with her over-stuffed pack, the look on the boy's face framed in the doorway—what was his name?—not as excited as she had hoped. The job ended up falling through.

What did Linnet like? She liked the look of the alpine line on the mountains, its natural evenness. Earth's precise measurement. She liked how wild thyme grew next to the vineyards outside of town and that's what gave the wine that deep herby taste. She had never discerned that taste in the wine, but it was enough just to know. Linnet liked Rey. She reminded her of a movie character but she couldn't say which one. Rey took a swig of rum.

'You know what's the ugliest colour?' Rey looked at Linnet. In the summer it didn't get truly dark till after 10pm, and right now they were in the shadowless blue hour of 9.30. The magic hour. The orange-then-pink setting light had already capped the mountains and faded. Linnet could look at Rey without squinting. Everyone looked younger at this time of night. And for the first time in a long time, Linnet felt young. She felt something being released into the air and down to the town below—something that felt like anger. It felt like rising and falling at the same time.

'Gold is the ugliest colour, no matter what country you're in. Did you know that with all the gold that was in California, there is still more gold in this little city, in this crystal-clear lake? It's just not commercially viable to mine it any more. They make their money in other ways. It's about assigning value. Soon, a few of the billionaires who live here are going to get together and make the next version of gold. Do you know what that is? A plasma colony. And young, poor people like you and me will work there giving them blood so they can live forever.'

The rum was sweet and bitter. Linnet thought that even if the gold was forgotten, the rich could still sense it. They were attracted to it, the smell of beauty tinged with gold. The smell of that kind of beauty was different to Linnet. What she smelled in the hotel mornings with the windows open to the rose-hued sky over the lakes was the vomit she cleaned up in the bathroom after working eighteen straight days over Christmas, the half-drunk bottles of Patron and sticky cheese boards, grapes and olives crushed into the grooves of the minimalist furniture and that protein-smell of semen.

They sat in the purple-dark. It was close to midnight. Some of Rey's friends had driven up and people were walking with their dogs and beers in their pockets. They had come for the fireworks, too. Rey popped open the champagne and poured sparkling gold swigs into everyone's cups. Rey put her arm around Linnet and rested her head on her shoulder. 'My pal Linnet,' she smiled. Linnet smiled back. She knew the fireworks would bloom at any moment, but for now all she could see were the bright headlights of cars moving quickly around the bends, flashing behind a corner or a crop of half-lit mansions, in a sure and steady progression. They could have been winding around the hills of California, through Monterey and San Bernardino in the strange Santa Ana winds she read about, headed towards whatever untold misfortune all linked through gold's past. In that moment she wasn't in Queenstown; if she closed her eyes she was in the emptied Sierra Nevadas or sitting on the Santa Monica hills, knowing that even though a vast desert, the west, was behind her, beyond that was infinitely more in every direction.

JADE RIORDAN

Night Builds Her Secret Town

the irises' *azure twilight* telescoping
away through the *same sky* of pupil-dark
to a small, half-known universe. Adjust
the view & falling stars streak like street
lamp glow (*the glow/ Of joy like dawning*)
between sturdy skyscraper walls of sulci.
Blink west like setting sun to the emptiest
ocean of space. Look again, a hundred
billion Yggdrasils dendrite-root & soft-talk-
tendril uptown, downtown, across town.
My every thought an *ominous dream*
echoing in the sap/ bark/ exhales lingering
between branches. My thoughts *bubbles*
... in an opal birdbath, a pair of hands cold
against a windowpane, a welcome mat,
a locked door, locked backdoor, a skeleton
key left *on those starry coasts* as twilight
lays the foundations & night gathers
her tools.

– The title of this poem and words in italics are quoted from
the poem 'Ghosts' by Robin Hyde.

Weightlessness

I've envied poems where fathers succumb to liver cancer
at seventy, a heart attack at fifty-five, these fathers
converted into a favourite tree in the family garden
or embodied via an old dinner suit. I've searched for
a working metaphor for you, something concrete, but find
you lack even the capacity to faintly dent soft furnishings.
Your winter work coat, black wool, knee length, has vanished.
So have your work shoes. Your spectacles, black-rimmed,
square-framed. Your tan leather briefcase. Your eyes.

Ah no, your son has those. That's true.
As I have copies of your teeth
in my mouth—a gentle dentist once offered
to fix them for me. I don't have
the sensation of your unshaven cheek against my face,
a feel for the specific way your body moved when walking,
any idea of how your mouth worked when you talked,
the sound of your voice, nor the ability
to imagine what you might have said about
all this. You have become the closest thing
to a man who never existed that a man who once lived can be.

EMIL McAVOY

Basement Biopsies

Established in 1945, New Zealand's National Publicity Studios (NPS) developed an arsenal of images to promote national identity, trade, and tourism—soft propaganda. NPS images are now largely invisible, redundant, displaced by new images compatible with current needs (although doubtless just as ideologically loaded). When Emil McAvoy trawled the NPS archive he found photos documenting old promotional displays. They may have whet appetites in their day, but these displays now seem clunky, corny, and forlorn.

In 2018 McAvoy presented a selection of the photos under the title *The National Basement* in the City Gallery Wellington show *This Is New Zealand*. His artistic contribution lay in his selection and loving digital restoration of the images, in reframing them and making them public.

Here, he crops multiple details from one photo—showing 'Building a Nation', a display from the late 1950s—while withholding the big picture. We see dated images and tired promo copy—selling a New Zealand that can no longer be bought (or bought into). We notice the old-fashioned eyelets the panels were hung from, the quaint suitcases they packed away into, and illegible incidental clutter. McAvoy calls his details 'biopsies', as if sampling from a larger image to determine the presence, cause, or extent of a disease. The devil is in the detail.

—Robert Leonard

Original image: New Zealand: 'Building a Nation' display
Photographer: Bruce Clark, 1959
National Publicity Studios, New Zealand government, AAQT 6401, A56730, Archives New Zealand, Department of Internal Affairs Te Tari Taiwhenua

Robert Leonard is chief curator at City Gallery Wellington.

Building a Nation

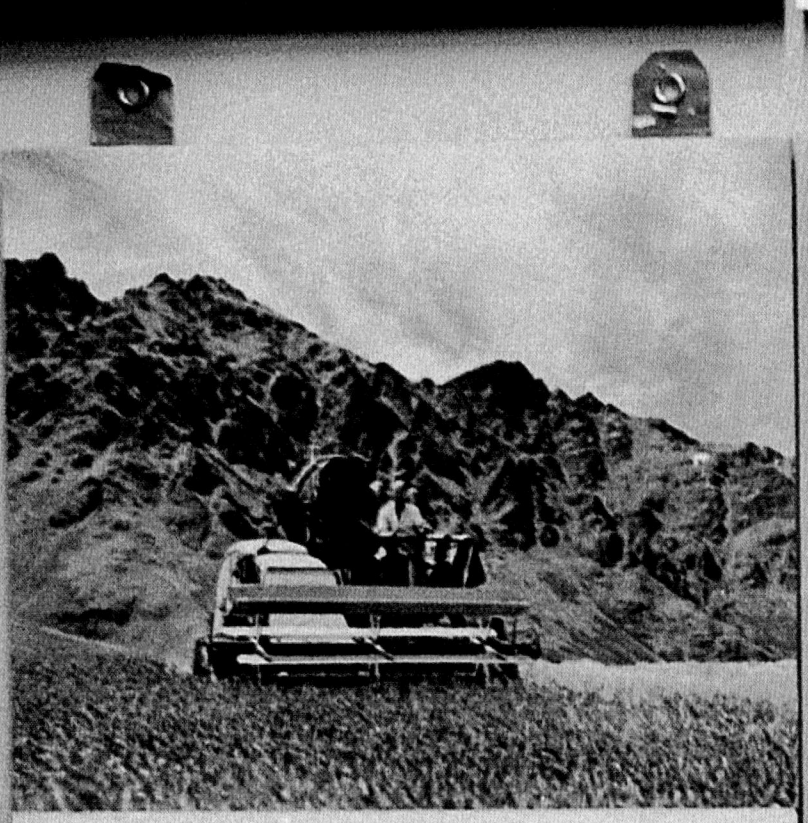

9.

GATHERING THE GRAIN

Wheat is harvested with a self-propelled header-harvester on this South Island farm. A wide range of annual crops are grown in New Zealand.

New Zealand is a young nation and is growing fast. Population doubled in the first half of this century. Production per head of population increased by half in just over a quarter of a century. And exports are up by half in the last 20 years.

Organised settlement and development have been under way for only 120 years, and in this time a modern welfare state has been created. Now, the rapid pace of economic development continues so that New Zealand can maintain high living standards for her own increasing population and help meet the needs of her neighbours throughout the world.

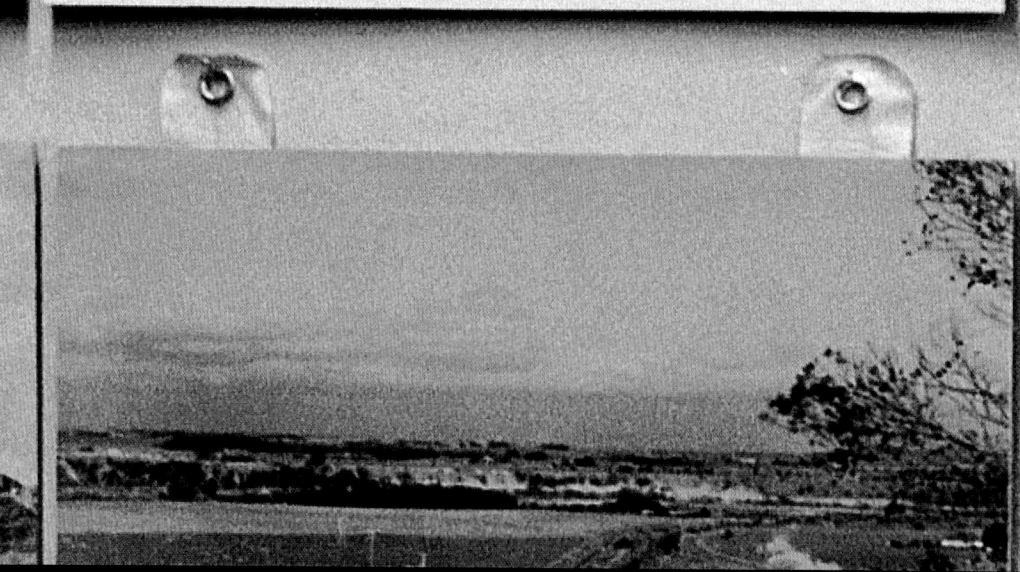

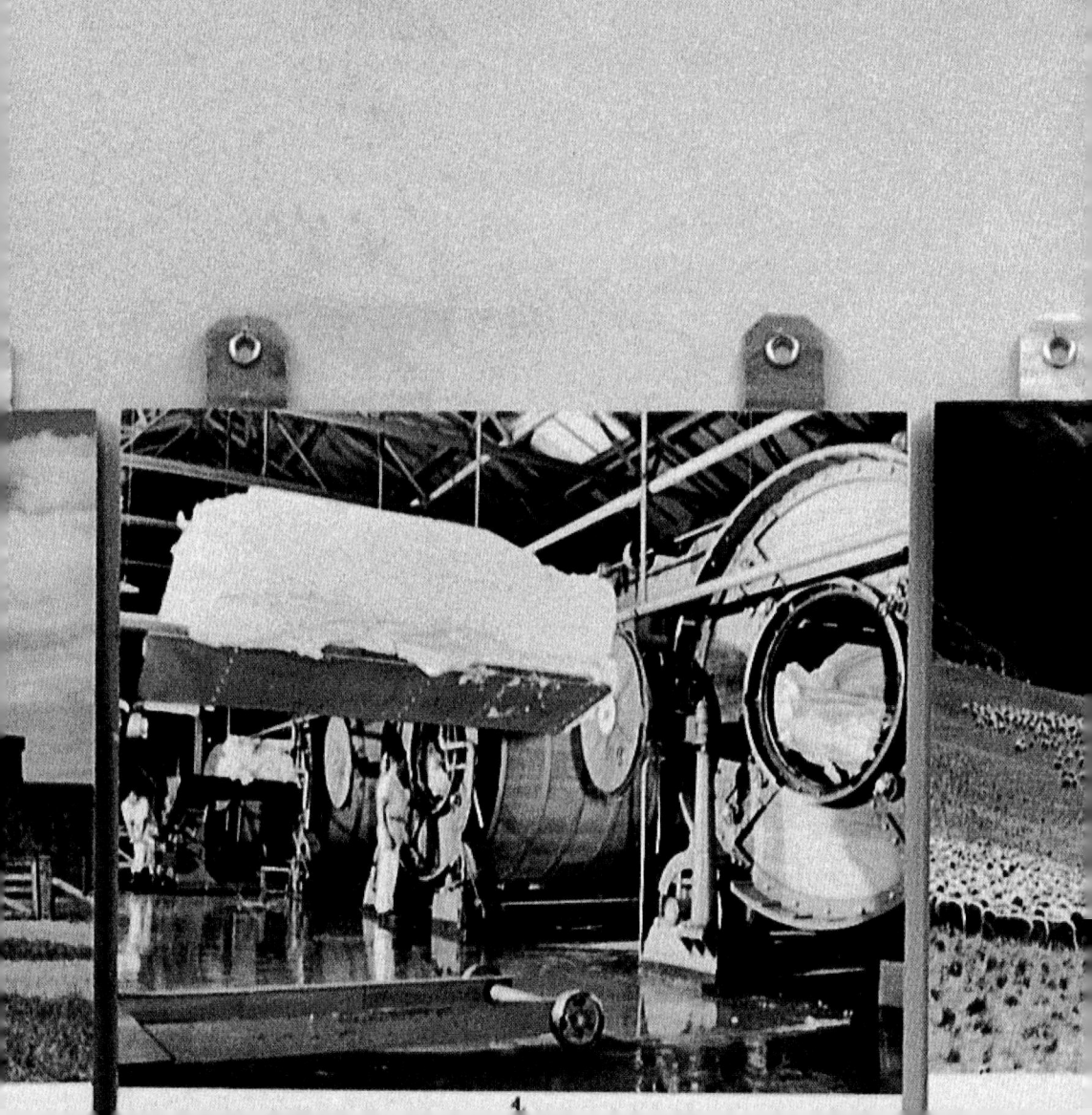

4

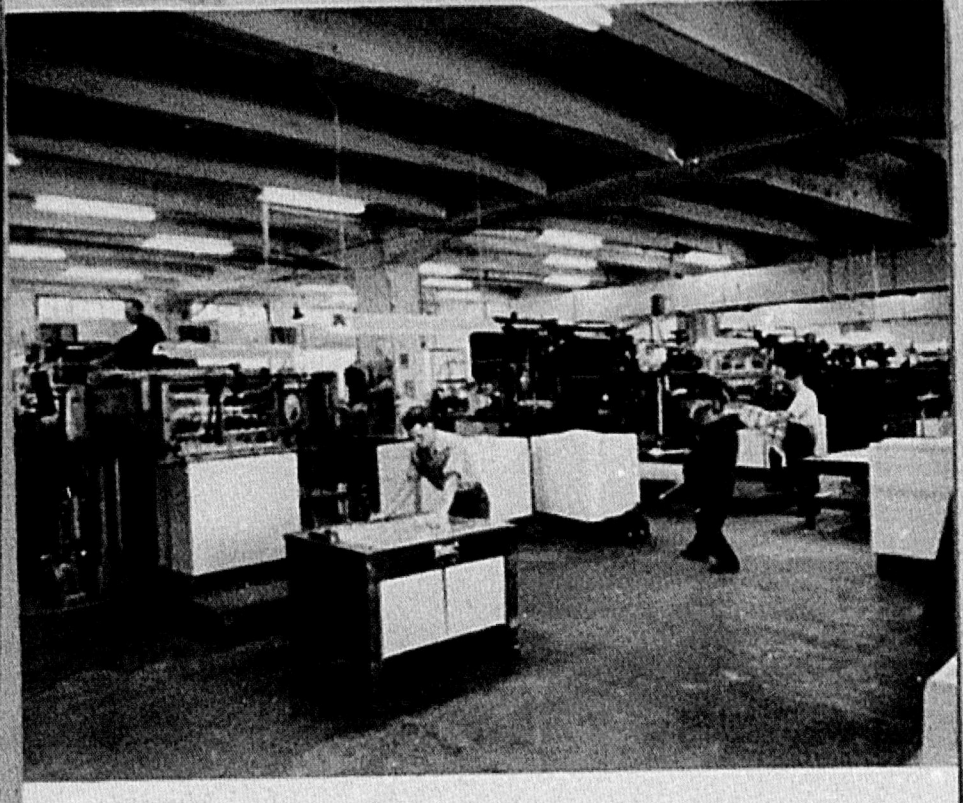

30.

MAGAZINES IN THE MAKING

From printing shops like this there is a constant flow of material to
inform and entertain the people of New Zealand.

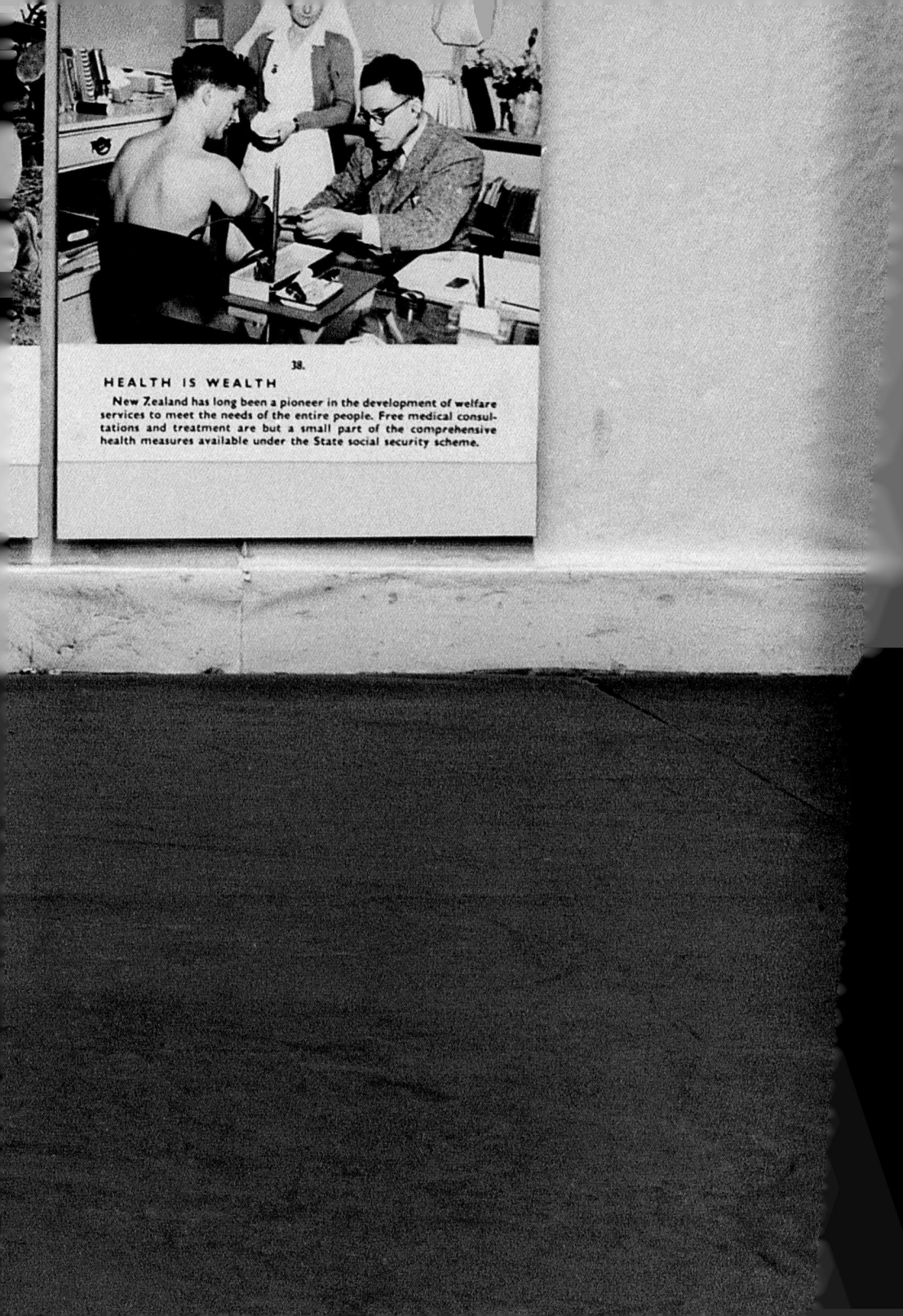

38.

HEALTH IS WEALTH

New Zealand has long been a pioneer in the development of welfare services to meet the needs of the entire people. Free medical consultations and treatment are but a small part of the comprehensive health measures available under the State social security scheme.

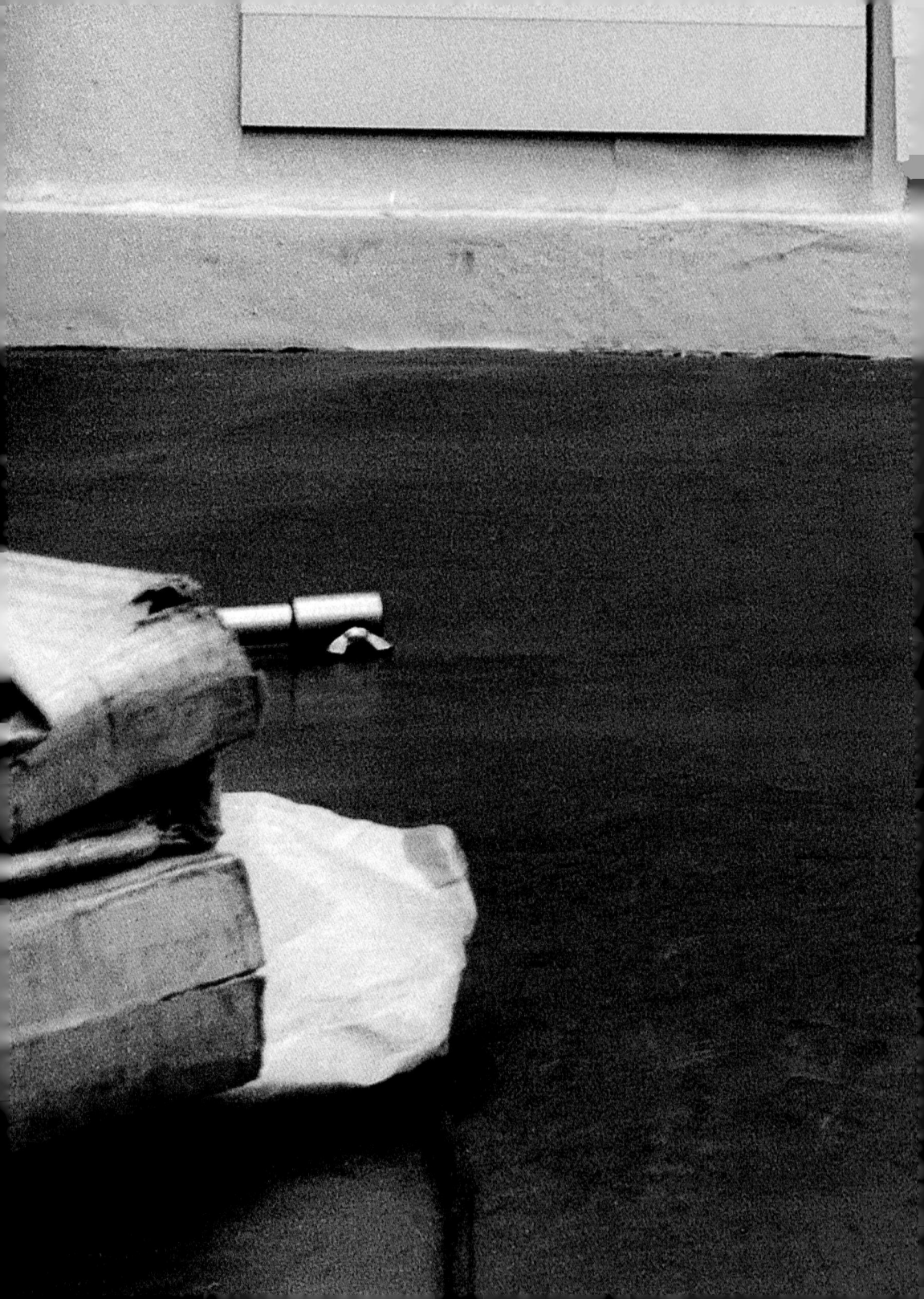

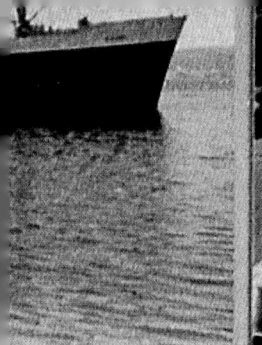

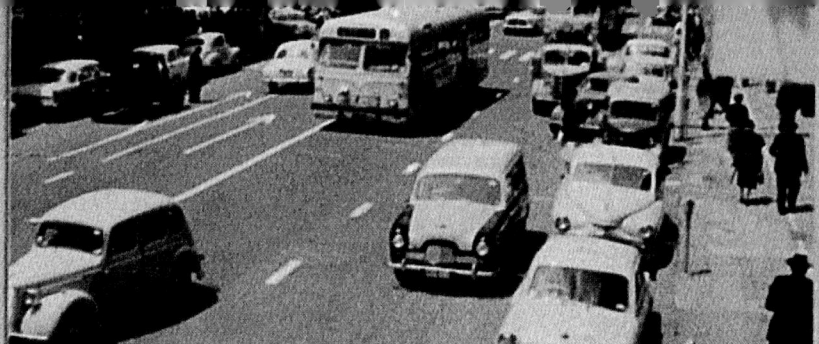

27.

A NATION ON WHEELS

The main street of Auckland, New Zealand's biggest city. Throughout the whole country there is a ratio of one motor vehicle to every three people, the third highest rate in the world.

-night passenger
dslands. A hard-
al service round

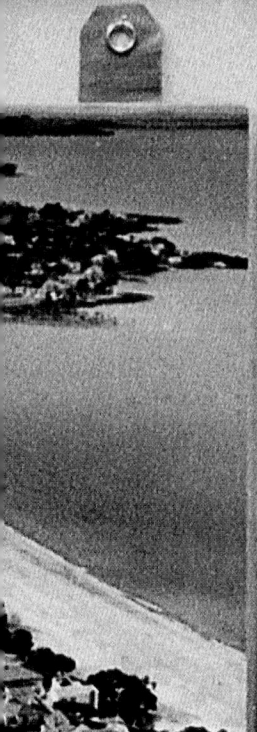

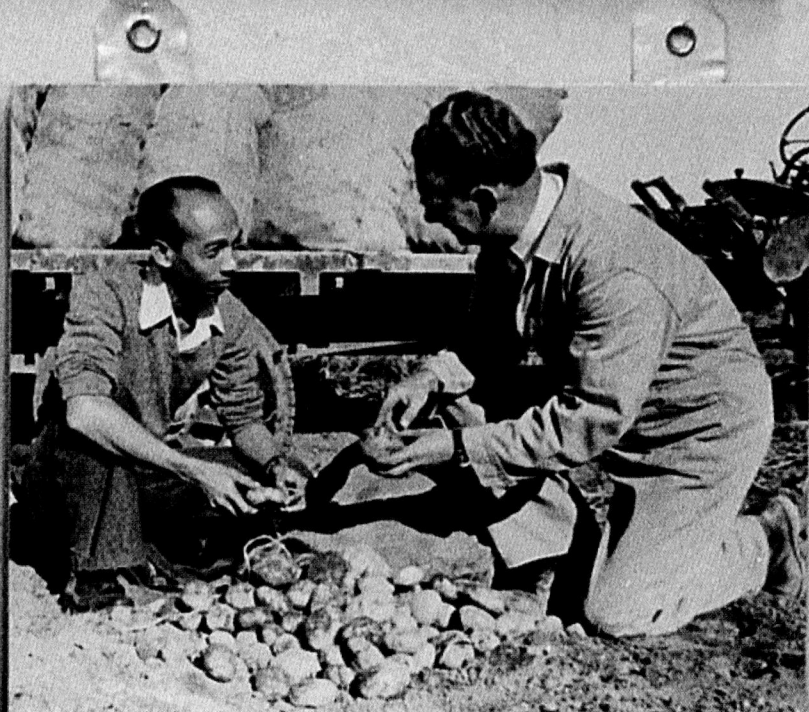

37.

ASIANS COME TO LEARN

New Zealand shares its fine facilities for agricultural education with students from abroad. This Colombo Plan student from Java studies at Canterbury Agricultural College, one of two such colleges of the University of New Zealand.

are in Auckland,
d's largest city.

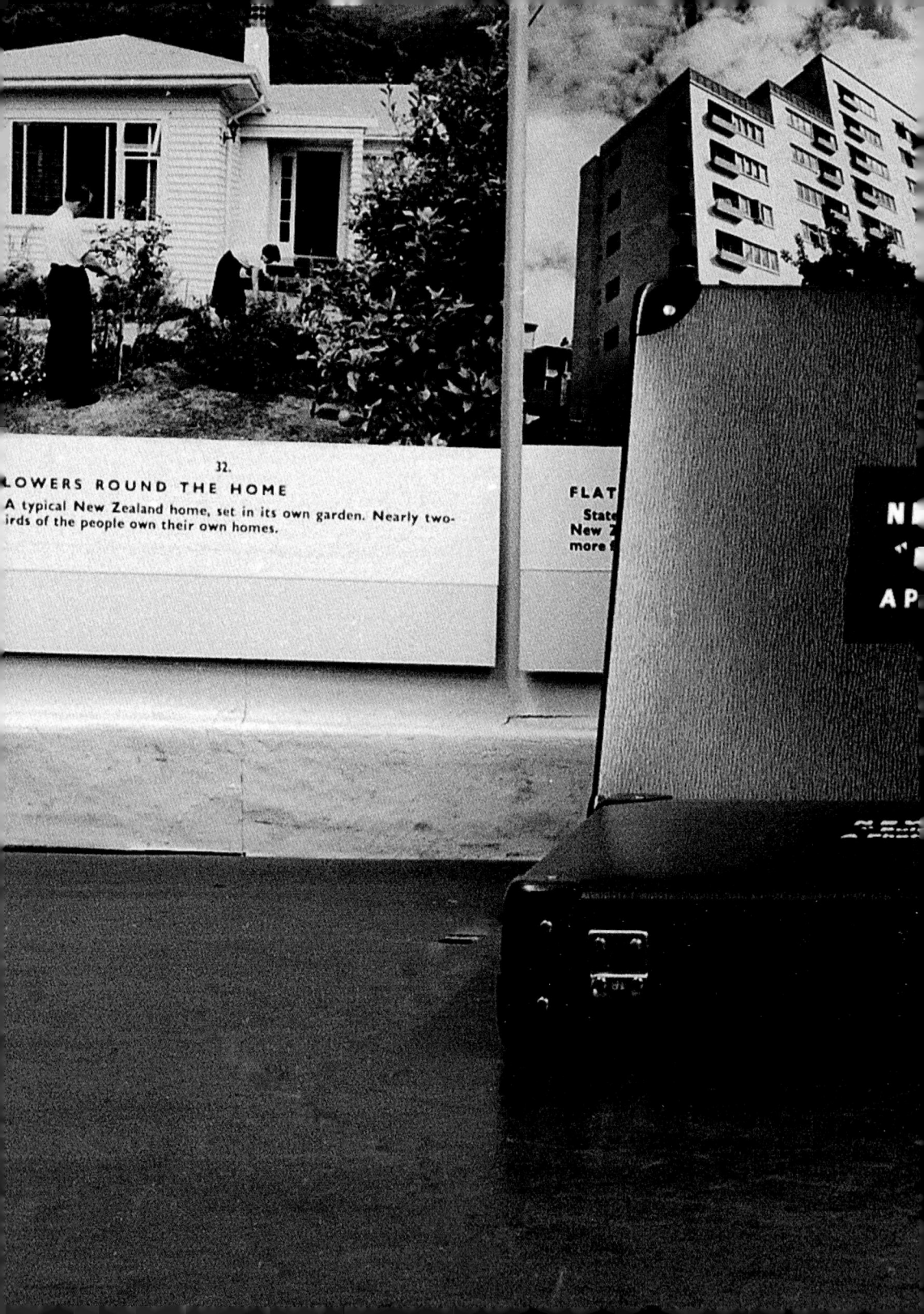

32.

LOWERS ROUND THE HOME

A typical New Zealand home, set in its own garden. Nearly two-irds of the people own their own homes.

FLAT

State

New Z

more

N

A P

JANET CHARMAN

selfie

used to be quicksilver
now when i pee
it's like drawing deep
conversation
out of me

notice the lunar skin
my limbs
spotted with the salt stains of torched summers

if i twist
there are dry chocolate ridges
i sometimes bite
in remembered sweetness

i do have these
nice suckling flabs o' breast
but years of trousers have walked away
with the hair on my legs

one tuft at the cleft
ornaments
the harbour of my hips

and time for my hunch
that short story of my mother's horror of her height
as i grew
i told it too

on my face
this feeling mask i can't put off

though when my eyes read
my brain denies
the blurred view of the right
and only accepts
the sharper counsel of the left

war memorial at Kohukohu

an arc of names
where the shock of brothers
is engraved with the dead

rain begins
pelting
down the jetty
to sit with the storm
in the passenger shed

we each remember differently she said

—my uncle knew i was filming
but he wanted it
told

how in front of him
and his little brother and sisters
their mother was attacked

when the soldiers left
she would have drowned
if from the bank they hadn't begged

the river runs into the harbour
the tide
brings her back

Lewis

I know I've been through here before, in youth
I roll my eyes at my young self, she who had her

but my eyes are wide, wider surely I
hand on her boyfriend's shoulder, his shirt was blue

have never seen this gold light lay down
I drove not seeing not seeing not seeing, what

valleys and bright wings splayed to sharp green hills
is this place?

PETER LE BAIGE

what she knows

wayfaring seed
of the wayfarer
bush
rested here
on the way to
some new earth
took root for
better or worse
in against the brick
a bush that houses
Little Cat the
pocket map
of tiger.
here behind
the grass
what does
Little Cat
know?
the thread of
cool that runs
along that
painted brick out
of the glaring
summer sky,
the things
she counts out
between
the leaves and
leaf shadow

like tabby mottle
over her,
the hop of bird,
deliciously
in sight,
the fumbled
pebble crawl
of beetle, the
ragged battering
wing of white
butterfly tossing
its talcum dust
against leaf
and web,
the soil's warmth
under paw, the
dry grass scratched
across her view
grass that frames her
face like a pastel vision
of Odilon Redon
floating through
its wreath.
the clouds that
are hardly there
above
a milk spilt
down the sky
and dried
away,
Little Cat
stays to know
these things her
given right,
the directions

of her senses
given in
that pocket
map of
tiger
she carries
in her
purse of
self

JANET WAINSCOTT

Ginevra Views Her Portrait

They'll read sadness
in my eyes, attribute this to barrenness,
assume I lived a life confined, nothing more
than my husband's chattel. In the future

a poet will ask forgiveness for eating plums
someone else, his wife, it seems,
had set aside for herself. So little
a wife may claim, but I

I am a poet; I roam free within
the palazzos of Florence and remain
singular. I devour pomegranates
but bear no fruit of my own.

It unsettles people
this childlessness, this
untamedness. *I ask your forgiveness. I am*
a mountain tiger.

*Ginevra de' Benci was the subject of a portrait by Leonardo da Vinci. Ginevra wrote poetry and the only line of hers that survives is: 'I ask your forgiveness. I am a mountain tiger.'

Being Sonya

Sonya's pregnant—that's what she told Ian anyway—but it's slow being home all day, so she's started taking the Tramadol prescribed following his accident. Now it's mid-morning and she swallows one of the white/blue capsules with the last of her coffee.

Along with her mug there are a few dishes left from breakfast so she runs hot water in the sink, adds detergent, and gets to work with the long-handled brush. The remains of Ian's bircher—since finding out, he's cut back on sugar and they've started walking more. She finishes, leaving the dishes draining in the low winter sun.

Out there is a gully of native bush and then two brick houses at the end of a cul-de-sac. Along from the cul-de-sac is a playground Sonya's been walking to every morning, waiting on her high. Drying her hands, she goes through their small rented villa. Updated bathroom, updated open-plan kitchen/living area, while the rest of the house is pretty much just two high-ceilinged bedrooms off the hallway.

Down the hall and out the front door in Ian's puffer jacket, up concrete steps to the footpath. No cars or people. Faintly, from the direction of Highgate, a siren. From here the view is of harbour, stadium and the tall beige buildings around the hospital. Tiny cars wheel the peninsula road. Two tugs motor out of sight. Low light from a sun now buried beneath grey. Work thinks she has had a miscarriage. She described it in her email as traumatic both physically and psychologically. Subject line: Indefinite Leave Required. She starts walking. Across the road, behind netting on the footpath side of a hedge, chickens move about.

Last night Ian asked, 'When will you get bigger?'

They were on the couch, and before she could answer he'd ducked his smiling face to her belly, placing his ear as if listening for a heart.

Lovely Ian. Hard-working, honest and determined to be a really good dad. She hadn't wanted to tell him she couldn't face going to work, she couldn't cope. Lies had been such a big part of her twenties and so here she is, comfortable for now in the gentle, harmless section of her deceit.

But a knife-man couldn't make her take another call. The Dunedin branch of the ACC call centre. Tradies shouting about their shoulder injuries being declined cover, callers with their Sensitive Claim letters asking how the government can help them through. Upbeat team leaders in sweat-stained shirts. Graduates saving for OEs. Nervy, worn-out mums returning to the workforce. Sonya used to throw up before shifts; she'd started hanging up on callers. No way is she going back.

Walking along the road, watching her shoes rise and fall, not high yet, but aware it won't be long. A man up a ladder, preparing a house for paint. His dragon breath. The shriek of the tool he's using. More sirens—multiple vehicles?—closer and louder. When she gets home she'll put a beer in the freezer with a glass, have a long, ultra-hot shower and then sit on the couch drinking. Tramadol brings delicious thirst. Also, nausea and itching. Best is the euphoria. Just *being* Sonya, it feels so good. What a good catch she's become. The nice feeling vacuuming puts in her arm muscles. And the other day, working that herb butter under the skin of that chicken, coaxing it over the breast, down into its wing pits. Cresting the hill, past the workmen, past a gutter bulging with brown leaves big as dinner plates, past the big rocks placed to keep car-hoons off the playground, and onto the playground itself. Swings, two old-fashioned see-saws, red monkey bars.

'The best chicken ever!' was what Ian had said about that bird.

Since she and Ian have been together her strengths have increased. Cooking, obviously, but also sticking to things—twelve months she was at ACC.

There's a grass bank before a narrow road that disappears into the town belt. She sits on a bench seat as two vans drive the curve of the broader main road. Beyond them is a soccer field, shrubs, and then more of the town belt. Out of nowhere a man's walking a little dog.

'Hi,' he says.

Sonya sits forward on the seat with her hands on the cold wood like in her mind is a plan to stand.

'Hi.'

He passes and she sits back. A red helicopter's out over the harbour.

Last night, sex made a good distraction from Ian's weight question. Instead of answering she'd just changed her couch position and kissed him deeply. Her orgasm was blunted a little by the Tramadol, or maybe it was Ian not being so determined—near where things got important he'd eased, asking if what he was doing was okay, if it wasn't too rough.

The obvious way out of the pregnancy thing is to invent a miscarriage. But how about getting pregnant? There was no contraception last night. Why would there be? Clearly Ian's keen. Clearly he's desperate to get down to BabyMart or wherever and start spending. Some of the maths wouldn't make sense, but she could blur that easily enough, she's so decisive when it comes to lying.

Interrupting her thoughts, timing their arrival with her first awareness of the drug, three police cars come from three different directions, parking in a place where buses turn at the bottom of the bank. Police people get out quickly from two cars and go to the window of the third. Then they return to their own vehicles and drive away in different directions, while the third car stays, its lights silently rippling.

Sonya watches. Wouldn't very dry champagne be nice? With Ian; yes, she genuinely wishes he was here. And feeling so sure about that makes it even more pleasurable to imagine. He's fast with jokes in these situations. Physically he's nimble and strong, and with words he's the same. Lately—it's not something they've discussed—he's started wearing his hair up and back from his forehead. She'll ask him about it over dinner. It's the sort of thing around which he'll sling a good joke. She gives herself back to the surrounds, but it's hard to ignore the police car. The word sting comes into her mind. Not as in wasp, but some sort of sneaky operation. She closes her eyes and sits right back, opening them on seagulls—black ticks—soaring.

Up there with them is a disc of moon. Pocked in the same way fat pocks salami. The moon would be close to the colour of that fat. She loves Ian and wants to be with him. Well, a version of herself is in love and wants to stay that way. To buy a house with Ian. To have a child—or children, see them here, at this very park, swinging together—with him. She scratches her hand and then reaches up under the breast of his jacket to scratch around the edge of her bra. To get older and older in his company.

Get pregnant then? Maybe the reason she's parked herself here is some kind of sign. Or maybe what she's doing with this lie is breaking them up? She did way worse with Gregor. Starting the lie off when they were living in Te Anau and really twisting the knife after he'd covered the cost of their move to Tauranga.

'New Zealand,' she says, thinking about the length of two islands while watching the police car, which, lights included, is now totally idle.

What could be going on around this nice neighbourhood?

'Someone left their hair-dryer on ...' she says, looking over her shoulder to see if anyone's caught the joke.

But there's no one except the cold wind in the grass and a selection of daisies, plus those yellow ones that aren't buttercups. Could she bouquet them up for Ian? The thought is dismissed. She's confident in overseeing the addling impact of Tramadol. No way is she one of those smelly druggie types you see around.

Home. Ah, home. Down the concrete steps and through the front door which the wind has opened for her. Straight from the pantry to the freezer with the beer and then into the bathroom where she undresses, folding each item onto the toilet seat while steam fills the room, sucking fast through the open window.

She hasn't really told Ian much about her twenties. I drank too much, moving from one town to another. I had a lot of relationships with unsuitable people. That's as detailed as it got. Violence happened back then though. Against her, and by her.

Acting on that memory—having just stood under the water until now—she sets to with Ian's shower brush. Scouring her legs, reaching back over each shoulder to go up and down over her lumbar area. Then choking it below the neck she gets about her arms. Finished, her skin crimson with the attention, she goes back to hanging under the hot water like a figure on a mobile.

Mum's to blame. Dying, you know, in my late teens. It left my boat a little rudderless. How many conversations in pubs and bars had she inserted that into? Rudderless. A way to get in. A way of letting another person know she wasn't in control, that she was up for anything. That word and her smile—the way she could sparkle her eyes, people were so easily convinced they mattered.

'Your eyes,' Ian would say. 'Jesus, they detonate.'

Noise comes from one of the bedrooms. Wind under the iron roof. Ian's been up there with rat traps. She flicks the shower dial to cold and, raising her arms, lets the cold cross her armpits. Then she turns slowly, stops and turns back, letting every part of her taste it. Ian introduced her to this—a blast of cold after the heat.

'Brings you alive,' he'd say, sliding soapy hands over her waist.

Another of the things that turns him on is when his financial adviser sends details about his portfolio. Graphs inserted into quarterly reports. Heavy, insistent language about yields and profits. He doesn't have much in there yet, but since Sonya's known him it's almost doubled. He's good with money. He works hard. Not that he's a National or ACT voter—he cares about people, he's against inequality; also in the mail they get information about a boy in Bangladesh he's been supporting since before he met Sonya.

'I just want to be the best version of myself,' he said once, 'which is where you come in.'

Sonya gets out of the shower. With his soft charcoal-coloured towel she pats at the drops on her skin. Why didn't she just tell him she couldn't handle the call centre? He would have understood. Probably he would have been encouraging. Some sort of relationship-building interaction might have taken place. No matter. She'll ease her way through, emerging with those daisies in her hair.

Outside are more sirens and then another round of the noise. A rattling—from one of the bedrooms? Has a bird got in? Is Ian home? Ian with his wonderfully mean-looking mouth—the only tough part of him. That would be a bind—if he came in while she was having beer. Defend drinking while pregnant or admit to lying ...

Not that she couldn't handle it. What did someone say once? She was both snake and charmer. Coming to full height, she wraps herself in the towel and goes into the hall.

'Ian?'

The tone of her voice—a little panicked—makes her smile.

'Ian?'

This time it comes out better, but there's no response. Their bedroom's cold and she needs to make the bed. No Ian though. She goes back into the hall where a draught's at her heels. Into the spare bedroom. Ian's exercycle and the poster of the man with a beard standing beside an old-fashioned saw. Nothing in here but the dust and the cold wooden floor beneath her feet. Courtesy of the Tramadol there's a little sea-sickness, but mostly Sonya feels wonderful.

'Beer o'clock,' she says to the sawyer.

Sitting on the couch, pouring beer into the frosty glass, looking up to see a kererū, wings tucked, missiling past. Raising her glass to the bird, she lets the nearly frozen liquid slide into her mouth, holds it a moment exploring— citrus against malt—and then swallows. And right then, as the beer goes down, there are footsteps.

'Ian?'

Beer comes out her mouth as she makes his name. She thinks of where she could hide the glass but then a woman's there, looking.

Big nostrils. Very dirty shoes. A straight back.

There's quiet as they look at each other. Then Sonya goes, 'Hi?' at the same time the woman goes, 'Is this your house?'

'Umm, yeah?'

Confused, Sonya's thinking back to last night/this morning, trying to locate memories of Ian saying something that might explain a visitor. Instead what she remembers is her old life. It was chaotic like this—random people, scary people. Not that this woman's scary. Mid-fifties and, other than the shoes, well-dressed. Tidy trousers, a fitted jersey—clothes you might see on one of the golf courses around here.

Sonya stands with her beer. It's okay, this interruption. The past has taught her she can handle pretty much anything. It would be better to be dressed though. 'Are you here for Ian?' she asks.

Golf-lady's big boned but Sonya would be stronger—she's sure of that. Ha! If it comes down to anything, she won't be worried.

As if sensing something relaxed in Sonya, the woman exhales, and like it's the punchline of some weird knock-knock joke, goes, 'Ian? Ian who? Is this his house?'

Thinking of another explanation for her presence, Sonya uses a harder voice, 'Why are you here?'

Because ACC employs investigators. Occasionally you got calls from people keen on dobbing in clients they thought were rorting the system. The neighbour with the 'bad back' sighted painting his roof. The hairdresser with RSI doing cuts in her kitchen. Stuff like that. Would work have sent this woman to verify her miscarriage? You couldn't put anything past the Corporation.

But the woman's ignoring Sonya. She's stepped away to look around. The woodburner, the antique fire tools hung there. Neatly stacked wood. Framed photos on the fireplace of Ian and Sonya holidaying on Banks Peninsula.

'I used to live here,' goes the woman.

Lightness returns and Sonya takes a good long drink. It's her house after all. 'And you've still got a key?'

The woman ignores the sarcasm.

'With my husband. With our three-year-old.'

'Hmm.'

'The door was open,' goes the woman, seeming to notice the beer for the first time, looking at Sonya a certain way.

'And what? You walk into any old house where a door's open?'

Sonya says it meanly. Then straightaway, embarrassed—Ian, no doubt, would have been overly polite; already he would have made coffee and shown her around, asking after their history—she starts to follow with something about getting dressed. But before she does the woman says, 'Since my diagnosis, I seem to have dispensed with some courtesies.'

'Sorry? I just—' Sonya points at the bathroom, as if the woman will know that's where her clothes are folded.

'Our son died in that room where you do your exercising.'

'Ian, umm—'

'He suffocated.'

'Suffocated?'

The woman nods. Then gestures at her chest and adds, 'Cancer. What I seem to be doing is going around the important places.'

'Shit,' says Sonya.

Smiling, the woman stays quiet, just raises her arms and then lets them flop to her side as if she couldn't have chosen a better word herself.

'We had bean bags.'

Sonya's dressed. They're both on the couch. Holding a beer, the woman's framing part of the carpet with her hands.

'Two of them there. My husband bought more beads for one of them—to fatten it out. Fatten it out ... the things you remember.'

Sonya drinks beer. 'Mmm.'

They don't know each other's names. The woman seems beyond that. She's here for her own thing—probably it wouldn't matter if Sonya was an octopus.

'So, he got this big plastic bag of beads and filled the bean bag, but the polystyrene things got all over the place, and by the time we hoovered them up, our son had taken the empty plastic bag into that front room of yours.'

Sonya finishes her beer. 'God.' A dead boy in there. The face. The mouth. On the underside of the plastic there would have been little breath drops. Like on a tent in the morning. Like the plastic was a wet windshield the boy was looking through. For Sonya, the inclination to say something tender crosses but, worried it won't come out right, she bites it back.

Then there's sustained knocking at the front door.

Many years later Sonya's shopping at the supermarket on Highgate—not far from that house she shared with Ian. She's convinced she's shrunk—though her doctor tells her she's the same height she's always been. Maybe it's your posture, he says, but there's nothing wrong with her posture. Looking at the bucket of free fruit supermarkets offer kids to keep them quiet, she again checks on her money card. She's forgotten her shopping list—her short-term memory is another complaint—but it's icy out there. No way was she scrabbling back up the hill.

'I'll figure it out, I'll free style,' she says, in a hard sort of voice, a voice asking for response. But people—the employee stacking celery, the bearded young man buying bananas—don't look over, let alone say anything.

A small number of groceries looks bad in a big trolley, so she's towing a basket on a plastic leash. Tinted glasses, an old knee-length coat, her long glossy hair tied in an ugly bun ... She loves it when people mistake her for sixty or whatever, for someone pension age. Loves the indignation she's able to strike back with. It's a trap she's still able to set.

Passing through PRODUCE, she aims at FISH.

Not that she can't still look good. Friday nights she transforms. Friday nights she's Wonder Woman. Careful makeup, arranging and then rearranging her few good clothes, then a taxi down to one of the Octagon pubs to watch and wait.

'Hello?' goes Sonya.

The fishmonger—a bouncy-looking creature with piercings—looks up from what she's doing. 'Sorry?'

'Gurnard, a fillet please.'

Sonya still tries to eat well. That's something she's carried over from Ian. Food was important to him (what was she making the night he confronted her?) and didn't she turn out to have a feeling for it! Following complicated recipes, shopping for good ingredients, thinking ahead in terms of *mise en place*.

The phrase—and the application of it to her old self—causes Sonya to bobble with pleasure and she sashays down the display. Whole monkfish, staring. Blue cod wings. Parsnip puree with pepper steak—that's what she'd been planning that night. The seasoned steak resting. The cream measured. The parsnip almost soft enough to blend. But before she could begin assembling, heavily down that old hallway he came, ignoring the food (ignoring the shiraz) and laying it all out: the Tramadol, the *non-pregnancy*. Of course he'd talked to the call centre—wasn't he an expert at getting to the bottom of things?

Irritated now, Sonya goes, 'Is it fresh today?'

'Sorry?' The fishmonger looks back over her shoulder.

'The fish—was it caught today?'

'It's all fresh,' she goes.

'That's not what I asked.'

The girl doesn't answer, just stays there wrapping the fish.

Trust issues—that's what Sonya has. It's what Ian talked about too—back that night of the parsnips and the break-up.

Faking it, the girl now hands Sonya her dinner with a smile. 'Have a nice day.'

Sonya doesn't respond, just bends to put the parcel in her basket and goes deeper into the supermarket.

The knocking that day—it had been two young cops. Neat beards, hair product, earnest—thinking of them now, their faces blend with Ian's, and what the police said was that a woman had been entering houses around the neighbourhood.

'We're concerned about a connection to an incident overnight when a dairy owner was threatened. Have you seen anything suspicious?'

Telling any sort of truth to the police was impossible—they were who lies were invented for—so she didn't give them anything. But it was a good neighbourhood, and she'd been stood in the doorway of a perfectly presentable villa so she'd been pleasant, even flirted a little.

MEAT now. Steaks, lamb, offal—a red road of it. She stands there swaying a little, trying to remember what was on her shopping list, unaware she's got her hand up over her throat as if someone might leap out of CEREALS with a knife.

On Octagon nights she always arrives early to get a table, sipping a drink, smiling, making sure she's open to anyone who might think to join her. Some nights pass and no one sits. Other nights a person might start with, 'Is this seat taken?' or 'Don't I know you from somewhere?'

Times are they'll get her a drink. Times are they'll have something to share.

'Times are …' says Sonya, moving on to stop at a display of pre-cooked rice, staring at the options like she's reading book spines at the library.

Rudderless—that's still something she might say. And there are four stories she leans on. One's what happened with Gregor. Another is the intruder. The other two are more recent, so she's not as confident in their delivery. Sometimes in telling them she'll slip a little, like a needle on an old record player, and end up mixing the stories. That happened recently and the man she'd been drinking with had slipped away. Slipped away from her table—'the way those fish would slide across this polished floor,' she says to the rice.

Really then, in truth, it's Gregor or the intruder. In the Gregor story she'll either be herself or Gregor—it depends on who she's talking to. Tailor your lies the way a tailor measures you for clothes. For example, a certain type of man—thick-necked—loves to hear that after talking to the police Sonya went back inside and challenged the tall woman, that a fight ensued involving a piece of that firewood and one of the fire tools. Other times she's left the intruder out altogether and claimed that dead child in the sawyer's room as her own. Playing for sympathy, your best approach is to deliver it lightly—people love it when you can go through something terrible with a bit of grace; they love it more when you can play down what's happened by saying something general about all people having their problems.

'What makes me so special?' says Sonya, entering WINE, and here's that feeling again—like it's all been laid out for her! All the proud little bottles, labels front and centre, are watching; the supermarket music—Celine Dion doing *Titanic*—is her soundtrack; and Sonya, Sonya with her tight package of fish in her otherwise empty basket is a glorious float at a street parade, she's a winning sailor on an America's Cup yacht, and any minute now she'll take off her glasses and raise her arms to the ticker-tape and the confetti.

MARY CRESSWELL

Primavera

They felt it first from the west
swooping in with the latest drones

brushing across skin lifting hair
like the force of a silent blast

      They could almost touch it
      it surrounded them and passed

      looking for other faces upturned
      small bodies crouching in small places

The children asked me what it was
      the breeze
            I said
                it's spring

They stared at me dumbfounded
      sting?
           like
              bees?

      The older ones explained:

Like sand flies up when rocks
explode on impact
            Your face feels it first
and then you know
you know now
      a whole new game is in the air

Kurangaituku

at primary school I saw a play
about Hatupatu and the bird-woman

the bird-woman had wings for arms
claws in place of fingers
lips formed into a beak

she wore a cloak of colourful feathers
her hair was on fire

nobody mentioned her name

*

Kurangaituku was friends with the birds
and small creatures of the forest
but she longed for something else

one day she heard the strange voice of a man
from high in the treetops

some say she abducted him
others say he was invited

stole her treasures and killed her friends
he stained her cave with blood and bone

when she discovered what he had done
her rage and grief became a weapon
guiding her closer to him

but Hatupatu was cunning
he led Kurangaituku to a hot-spring
where her half-bird body boiled

*

the story ends with her
sprawled out and lifeless
on the lacquered brown floors
of our school hall

PAOLO CACCIOPPOLI

Open House

Chained to his trolley, the mendicant sings
in a voice long left out in the rain and the wind,
stony as the pavements that he has been walking
yet skirted with moss and a chuckling of birdsong,
as though with the trees he were coming into spring
and an excess of sap. From time to time
he checks his belongings
with the unease of someone accustomed to losing
a little each day. A woman in a fur coat
keeps walking after the signal has changed
and he sings to her safety;
The cars halt in time, and he wheels himself on
with his bags of old papers and battered tins,
limping as if he had taken the hit
but the crowds brush him by.
There's no root could grow from his hoard of things.

JENI CURTIS

Never Draw the Blinds

Never draw the blinds on the insurrection of the heart:
love will arrive at any time; let it be felt,
let the voltage of the spirit spark
through the architecture of the veins. There are no faults,
no bundle of old doubts, as the pulse quickens for its part
despite the unfamiliarity of age. Bear its assault.

Never draw the blinds on the insurrection of the heart:
the body is fluent in the memory of love's craft
and, in its grain, emotions rise like yeast,
no stopper on the feelings from the past,
wheat or chaff, you already know this path;
you have eaten of this bread, know it may not last.

JODIE DALGLEISH

The Love of the Newcomer

I'm taking a turn around
my village each day, an immigrant
for change

in the sun's finest gauge
of roof-fall drawn onto bright walls; lintels drawn
by window shine; light's points falling

knit over cobbles, as everyone walks out with a dog.
I wander each stellar difference in my body's
curve, of chromatics and branches and coronae
and the new season's blooms that are

hooks, where every small token becomes
a course of events from arrival
to the superlative, of circling

birds on the updraft over the valley's
spire, white tips above the houses, a round
of fresh air on the skin, bent to 'here'
continuously.

The Long Game

The contents of this page are being extracted.
The long game. A log stacked on a log.
A process unfortunate and eerie
creates watcher and waiter. Don't
resist the exchange. Trace elements made
off by a rivercold burn. Prance,
a dancing word, twists in the gut, prickles
soles and lobes. Feet in water,
fleshstones filigreed by moss and fern.
Click and clatter of shifting urgencies. Bone
chilled witness, smooths to the running stream.
Precarious on your bed tonight, Maid of Stones,
beauty braced and balanced,
ankle deep in racketing current.

DAVID EGGLETON

Generations

Young moths rustle mottoes of dust under
hard rustle of flax, clusters of cracked pods.
An old wētā trawls a sea of forest fronds.
Wasps weave and wrap their pollen trails
over briars loaded with black blood drops
heavier than hearts can bear, for the trees
are our parents' parents, diving down
a millennium underground, bent round
and curled in a birth dream, till the years
unfold roots that twist out of rock fissures,
and climb as seedlings, tender, glowing,
to where bed springs rust in landfill dumps,
in slow tick of rains, and the sulphur creeks
bubble up their finest skim of green scum.

Catch

Herding drops of heavy rain,
paddocks settle in paspalum,
Clouds shroud macrocarpa.
The water flexes and wades,
and glides finger by finger,
to join more water, lush
over globed slither of rock,
past gnawed traceries of leaf,
swimming slowly to make
from swampy genesis a river.

CINDY BOTHA

A Milk-cow on Mother's Day

you stop
and search my face
across the wire
you've never

licked clean a glistening
newborn slipped
from your hips'
blood-hold

noses that knew instantly
each other's self
without soft nudge
or rasping tongue

I see your cargoes lost
and lost
the udder's futile basin
drained dry

see the empty space
that hefts you stumbling
searching
in the night

and bellows out of you
each calfless dawn

Rabbit Run

When he opens the curtains in the morning light and lets in the faint tang of frost, the rabbit is always there. Well, not always: he's recently become wary about the pitfalls of globalised statements. Invariably, then. Often. Mostly. Mostly, when he greets the day he is also greeting a fat black rabbit, who taunts him from what passes as a lawn, nibbling.

The kids think the rabbit is cool, is beautiful, is a magic lagomorph among the other biscuit brown streaks that litter the land, is 'Dad, can we *keeeeeeeeeep* him? *Pleeeeeeeeease?*'

Yeahnah. Pests. Scourge. Things you're supposed to shoot or poison. Things the regional council people count. And what would the boys say? Still, what would it take? Chicken wire, posts, old tent pegs to secure the bottom edges. A moveable pen, like they have for chickens. A rabbit-proof fence, but for keeping the predators in.

Pretty cute predator really, he thinks, blowing soft over the crema on his coffee. If he could get close enough, maybe it would have a little blond twitching nose. But whatever. They're not keeping it and that's final. Though it would be cheaper than the dog they also want.

Half an hour later the chicken wire is half-uncoiled on the lawn. He's surveying, patching gaps. Old tent poles. Pegs to slot down the sides of the wire. But maybe save it, right? Do it with the kids. Do the ouchy bits now, though. Pace its length, fold hexagons into right angles, loop the wire edges into a tangle, joined.

He climbs into the nearly-cage with his second coffee, rolls a smoke and Googles 'black rabbit' on his phone. Black Rabbit Pizza. Black Rabbit Bangalore, with a red upside-down teardrop locator. 'Power pop purveyors of

102

punk and garage.' 'Military garments, oriental tailoring and modern sportswear.' Nothing about magic on the lawn in the morning.

Once, while looking for a lost ring, he found a frog under a stone. Lurid green and yellow, big eyes as startled as his own, hiding in plain sight. Both of them stunned, frozen. He remembers the wanting, to put it in a jar. To show. To tell. But when he moved, stealthy as a small kid thinks he can, a flash of back legs and it was gone.

He crushes the end of the rollie over in the dregs of the cup and steps out over the wire. A loose edge nicks his jeans—when's he going to learn to wear work trou to work in? But there's only an hour now before picking up the kids. Where does the time go? No point in getting changed and getting changed.

In the car on the way home from kindy, he explains, his eyes catching theirs in the mirror. The kids argue, of course, over who gets to use the hammer first. He will have to split up the tent pegs into two exact piles so everything is fair and even. Perhaps they can count them out together. After they count out the pasta and fish fingers for dinner.

The tent poles go in easily, vertical, threaded. The kids hold the bottoms, turn about, and he guides the pole through from the top. The pegs are trickier and he ends up holding them while the mallet, hovering in two hands, strikes and strikes different somewheres in the vicinity of its target. Only one finger needs kissing better. And there it is. Square. Ish. Secure. Ish. Their own rabbit run.

Black rabbit invariably, mostly, often makes an appearance in the evenings, when the mountains are doing that triple-vista thing that makes him want to check the strength of his glasses or believe in a higher power, or both.

This night they plan to lure black rabbit, grab him quick, while he's distracted with vegetable scraps and song. The kids pick what they call the juiciest celery leaves and the softest carrot feathers and sing, pyjama bottoms on—'haere mai rāpeti, haere mai rāpeti, hae-re-mai,'—so black rabbit will know he's special and best. The sun slides behind pine trees and toetoe. They wait.

Rabbit

(*Ekphrastic poem after 'How to Explain Pictures to a Dead Hare' by Joseph Beuys*)

To speak your name aloud is unlucky
but there is a loophole; I murmur
that you are not a replacement rabbit.
Your split-lipped face and leather ears

cool faster than I can explain.
I draw your portrait. You resemble me,
face smeared with honey and gold,
feet shod one in iron, one in felt.

Thump with one, the other muffled.
I know the sound of your tread
although you will not walk.
beloved, beloved, beloved

I pencil in the hairs of downy fur
worn away here and there by the friction
of your bundled blankets. Your damage
held together, swaddled in my arms.

I Invite Myself Inside

You have not kissed me. I have not been kissed. The night approaches with the sound of starlings finding roost. And you have still not kissed me. I kissed myself in the mirror of myself to find the thread that connected me to the place where I knew what it meant to be someone after their own heart. Or hearts in the same shape. The shape of a heart is the fist. Gender is a cloud where no one exists as a real thing. We are all just the skin that covers our bodies underneath the clothes that cover us up. I've told you since I was eighteen that I'm not the same person I looked like I would be when my clothes aren't there. I've told you that the outside and the inside are not the same place even in a human body. You don't have to say my name. I don't have to know anything about you. Just say some of those words out loud and out loud and out loud. The horizon pretends to be flat because we can't believe the shape. My shape shifts as it is perceived. I'm perceived through several different moments in time at the same time. You know how to freeze-frame I know how to say abracadabra forwards and backwards and into the space above your head. Your head above me is hard to look at. Like everything that I've ever looked at I forget it only to remember it later. In the secret mythology of a self I write down everything. It rolls through me like the barrel of a zoetrope spinning and spinning and the horse moves inside me. And I am the horse. And the horse rolls its eyes right out of its head. I have kissed you but I don't remember. I have kissed you and I remember each dizzying moment. I have not kissed you and looking at your mouth in the dim light of dusk is invitation enough. I invite myself inside.

MICHAEL STEVEN

At Eastern Southland

Saturday. Beside a bridge where freighters
shift their tonnage through the province
I unpack the hard cargo of your last photo.
Your baseball cap wreathed by flowers
rests on a casket black as a polished piano.

This afternoon in the moonshiner's museum
I sipped plastic thimbles of mānuka spirits.
Folkways of Celtic colonial outlaws,
their descendants lay low in every suburb:
bedroom botanists, alchemists at hot stoves.

⋆

Time slows here to the pace of a breeze
jostling the heads of marram grasses.
An angler in waist-height rubber waders
threads his clear line to the grey river.
You're my third friend deducted this year.

As a garden of asbestos tumours flowered
in his lungs, one friend mutely syllabled,
'Text me, bro,' when our visit ended.
The next wrote, 'Hurry.' I was late again.
You did it at home. A euphemism: suddenly.

⋆

Silence sings along the bridge's red girders.
It sings through the cold stone arches.
It is singing on these blackened iron rails
bending back through hills and plains,
back to the city we wintered a new century.

We flinched while fixing at desolate tables
in rented kitchens. Springfield Road.
My shitty bedsitter on Worcester Street.
Days and nights: oblivion rehearsals.
You were my one call when I got busted.

*

Rolleston. My season inside a concrete slot.
I broke new fears. An older safecracker
took me under his wing. He had one lesson,
'Keep your head down. Borrow nothing.'
I read and taught myself to build sentences.

Beyond the boundary hush of the wire fence
freighters keened through dark paddocks.
I found a reprieve using words to order reality.
You dreamt sine waves and drum patterns.
The dance took you into breakbeat wormholes.

*

Winter's first word came with early frosts.
Diesel yellow dawns at New Brighton.
A streetlight bristled over my driveway.
You were moving away to get clean.
Our last hug smelled of skunk and tobacco.

I promised to call, to visit. In his car seat
your infant son cooed with the music
of knocking pistons in your idling sedan.
He has a brother. They are fatherless.
It is summer now and I will not find you.

*

Sandflies cloud the obdurate angler's form.
He raises his right arm over his head,
flicking the graphite rod into a lean arc.
The hook ripples the surface of grey water.
Silence is the last step in every sequence.

One suburb gives echo to another's boredom.
Soon the freighters will be moving again,
hauling the heart's hard cargo to a new city.
A timer clicks off and a world darkens.
Your silence goes on. It sings and it sings.

On a Mat at the Bottom of the World

At the bottom of the world we sat cross-legged with arms folded
on a mat behind the teacher who wore pink plastic pop beads,
matching bri-nylon twinset, a tweed skirt and see-through nylon stockings
as she played the piano and we sang, 'Oh Dear, What Can the Matter Be?'
Outside, flax blades clapped and the grey sea beyond the railway line
seethed in its own mist. We sang, 'Oh dear, what can the matter be?
Johnny's so long at the fair,' with me believing it to be a song about my cousin
Billy who had disappeared from home and nobody knew where he was
until he was found sleeping in his car, the one he always drove too fast
around corners. And the fair, I thought, was the one held every year
in the rec, with bagpipes, wood chopping and black-slippered dancers
dancing the Sword Dance on the empty deck of a truck. We sang,
'He promised to buy me a bunch of blue ribbons' just like the ribbon
on the hairclip Sandra Mason always wore in her dark hair
with its pale zigzag parting, like lightning. 'To tie up my bonny brown hair':
as brown as the acorns under the oak trees along Lattas' drive.
We sang, 'Dear, dear, what can the matter be'? on a mat
at the bottom of the world, as young Billy made his way back home
past the pig farm, the bracken and gorse. We sang on a mat
at the bottom of the world, sitting cross-legged with our arms folded
making our own world and never asking why, and if the teacher did know
what the matter was she never let on, in her pink plastic pop beads,
bri-nylon twinset, tweed skirt and, under her see-through nylons,
black leg hairs pressed flat into the shape of tiny question marks.

JOHN ALLISON

Experiment before Monet's Painting of Waterlilies

Simply think, here is a little square of blue, here an oblong of pink, here a streak of yellow, and paint it just as it appears to you …

—Claude Monet

Seen close up, it's just paint, a brush-stroked surface, thoroughly worked over. Really it's a mess, I think. Paint, just paint, in no apparent pattern.

Looking, I walk slowly backwards until suddenly it all coheres and the paint becomes a painting, that lovely image, waterlilies on a pond. It is wonderful. But when I walk towards it once again there's a point where the waterlilies disappear into abstract daubed shapes. I walk backwards again and there it is. Monet's painting of waterlilies.

So where is this happening? Where is the image? And how did the artist see it there while he was close up, painting it? Did it disappear for him into a little square of blue, an oblong of pink, a streak of yellow? Just that? In the end, did the waterlilies matter?

The image is not there upon the canvas, it is not the paint itself, it is not somehow coded and concealed within the painting's 'thingness', in that thickly textured substance on the surface of the canvas …

I walk forward, then back, looking harder. There is what is seen, and there is what is thought. Then there's that Romantic thing, *emotion recollected in tranquillity*. I wonder, just in passing as it were: if I could find the right distance in relation to my life, would everything then cohere?

LINDSAY RABBITT

Hush Puppies

Patti Smith owns a pair of Pope Benedict's slippers;
also a pair of Robert Mapplethorpe's.

I buy a new pair of slip-ons, Hush Puppies,
from Hannahs at Coastlands.

Outside the mall I discreetly slip the old pair
into a rubbish bin, and with a new spring

in my step comes an image
of an ice shelf, of an ice shelf calving.

LOUISE WALLACE

Tired Mothers

There are tired mothers everywhere.
I see that now because I am one.

Tired mothers in the kitchen
making tiny tuna croquettes.

Tired mothers finishing
folding all the washing.

Tired mothers running after their children
running towards the road.

The washing line was a joke obviously
because you'll never finish that.

There are even those mothers who say
they wouldn't change a thing for the world

and then you see the two dark wells
under their eyes and feel better.

Random observations don't make a good poem.
Things that make you go huh! are not enough.

But why shouldn't I get to be lazy
just because this poem is about kids?

We've all been to a documentary before
or seen some interesting street art, Darren.

Any of us could visit Kerouac's grave
and sit and play a miniature organ. But we don't.

Portal to the Stars

There was a time when I'd lie in my bed
and look out the window above it
to the whetū. I never knew
what the brightest ones were called.

Venus or Mars?
On clear nights I'd say to myself,
'I should ask him when he gets here,'
but I had other things on my mind by then.

The next morning he'd be gone.
Back to his other love,
taking the winding road
where Papatūānuku was reclaiming her skin.

In the brief moments before sleep,
eyes open to a thick blanket of secrets,
my breath and limbs were always
the same hefty stone.

Joan

(for Deborah)

They lay opposite
each other,
pumps pinging
in unison.
Joan, swamped
in a hug
of dyed fibre;
bruised wool
framing lemon
daffodils and a
rust-red sky
pearl-stitched
above Rangitoto.

I wonder if
she made it.

Bus Lament

I'm sorry for taking the bus, I'm sorry
for trumpeting my weeks of discontent
through piss-coloured stage lights
at open mics meant for grownups

I'm sorry for going to McDonald's;
for sliding my hands into the pockets
of golden-arched corporations & leaving
whole dollars there. I'm sorry

for all the fudged transactions &
the ugly looks & the lunchbreak where I
chipped off most of my
nail polish & told him to find
another café with less emotionally
invested baristas. I thought
about peeing in his cappuccino &
I thought about crying in his cappuccino &
instead I pressed my palm to the slowly
warming milk jug & did neither.

Gwen from work's nephew has
eight months to live, I heard her tell
somebody else & now I'm telling you. One
weekend morning the horn in my father's parked car
broke & it wailed through the hungover street
for forty-five minutes while neighbours
lined up outside. So I'm sorry for that, too, I guess,
or things that are similar to that.

I'm sorry for all the time I
wasted in wailing, for the eight-month
increments of bullshit for which
Gwen from work's nephew would
likely resent me.

Here is what mattered, after we didn't like
each other any more:
lacing my boots so tightly my feet
tingled. His hands in the dishwater & his eyes
anywhere but me. Gwen from work
offered to pass her flu on to him for me
& I pity anyone who has not known
such a glowing kindness. I apologised for
what I did not know & what I did not do,
over & over, until he seemed almost
innocent. This was wrong, whatever
that can mean. Nobody

gets out of anything ungrubby.
Mostly I am tired. Mostly I am sad
I will not see his cat again.

ZOË MEAGER

First Dispatch from the Front

This and that, this and that. She has a lot of this and that to do. Water this Boston-bird's-nest-maidenhair-rabbit's-foot fern, scrub that slow-cooking-toaster, that saucepan-sieve. She's got a tea towel that wants a stubborn sigh removed, and a politician in the attic who wants listening to, for one hour, two. She'll yank the ladder down and climb it and listen listen with this ear and listen listen with that, and he will smile spit shout and she will slip lit fireworks up his trouser leg and leave him to combust. Back downstairs she will fold the pinafores, fold the onesies, fold the silky-nightie-longjohn-fitted-sheet. She will switch the radio on and catch some of the news but only the highlights, because she's got a patient in the sleep-out who wants tending and there's a family of refugees in the living room who want and want and want, their boat spins in the middle of the carpet, sending up flares that burn the ceiling in the shapes of another language. She will side-step them to find a matriarch in the kitchen who wants the butter softened, who wants to press her palm into it and leave all five digits impressed there like tracks for blood to flow down. To a lost child in the hallway who needs comforting she will show garter-stocking-blanket stitch, and he will practise with clumsy fingers on his own liver but now there's a knocking at the door there's a knocking, a whole hospital waits outside with the smell of fluid inside-outness, and she will open up a crack and tell them *I've only room for a crutch*, but there's a knocking at the door there's a knocking, the sea is surging to come inside, and she will open up a crack and say *Please, I've only room for one thin starfish*, but there's a knocking at the door there's a knocking, firefighters have come to stop an ouroboros forest from devouring itself, and she will open up a crack and say, *Just hand me an axe. I've got to get back to the roses I've got growing in the walls.*

Miniature Worlds

Act One

The director is waiting for my script. He needs lines for an ingenue with waist-length hair who stands on tiptoes as if she is walking on knives. We have made a backdrop—a balustrade with a distant view of mountains and clouds, and in one of the wings a fold-out screen waits, painted to look like the windows of a palace. In the meantime, I am captured posing for a photograph on a swing beside a shed, fountain pen in one hand half concealed and a fairy-tale book in my lap. If I stare long enough without blinking, the lawn reveals itself as a jungle full of ant trails beneath the pale flowers of Onehunga weed and glistening brass shavings from my father's lathe. Sometimes I imagine movement under the azaleas: little arms, a foot. The theatre will seem like a wonderful game in fifty years' time after the hedge between the houses has gone, along with the smell of pee, the memory of a bruise on the director's cheek and the sight of his small pink penis, like a finger without a bone. His sideways glance. We had been hiding, shoulder against shoulder, dust from the path gritty inside my sandals, pee leaving a dark stain in the dirt, bees hovering in the hedge among its white flowers. I caught one in my hand and felt its thrumming.

Act Two

The ingenue has red hair and tiny breasts that feel like pearl beads inside her plastic chest and she wears a little white dress made of lace cut from a petticoat. We argued for days about her name: I had wanted Arriety, but in the end we chose Lola. Lola, with the simpering pout and a hole in her back where she might once have been attached like a maquette to a stand. She has lost her shoes. We discuss how to find more figures the same size as Lola and read alternate lines from a copy of Hamlet the director found on his father's bookshelf. When the lines don't go right across the page, it must be poetry. There might have been ten thousand Lolas once, maybe more. Someone will have glued eyelashes onto their soft, caramel-coloured faces, painting blue eyes or brown; each with a little dab of white. He holds Lola upside down and her dress falls over her head. Her little bead breasts have no nipples and there is nothing between her legs. Much later, we will seek each other out with a new script in which he slowly peels off all my clothes, folding them carefully onto a chair. Proscenium arch, apron, stage left. The bus ride home alone past flashing neon. His father watched us through the garage door, eye blinking like a shutter. Something captured.

Intermission

When the girl thinks about the theatre in the years to come, she will recall pencils as table legs, thimbles for cups. An eye at the door. Tiny things. Wooden chess pieces and the top hat, the iron, the little dog from a game of Monopoly. A blink. The smell of wood shavings, oil and cigarette smoke. How Lola could not stand by herself and the boy's father had her practise reading speeches from Hamlet while the boy painted scenery for the theatre. How they found a piece of fur in a box, skin gone hard and crackling, but they could lay it on the stage as if it were a rug in front of the leaded glass, the balustrade and the painted sky. Lola could lie on it, surrounded by tiny flowers, forget-me-nots and daisies. 'What, the fair Ophelia!' How she stumbled over the words, the book on the workbench propped up against the vice and how a moth was caught in a spiderweb. Gossamer. Her tongue lingering over the syllables. A sound like steam. It was easier to make tableaux than to move the actors about. The father made her keep one finger underneath the words and run the lines into each other. He might have stood very close or perhaps there wasn't much room. When it began to get dark she would go home but she could see the light in the garage from her bedroom window and the shadows of the boy and his father. An arm swinging. A hand. Like a movie with the sound turned off. She could not know then how it would all end.

Act Three
We had a windup gramophone and a collection of 78s. The needles came in a gold-coloured tin shaped like a pyramid. He drew black lines around Lola's eyes, twisting her head so that she looked Egyptian; arms and legs at right angles to her neck. Her bead breasts bare. I spirited a wooden camel and a set of elephants away from the bookcase at home. Lola was taller than the elephants so they were always upstage beside the pyramid. The tone arm of the gramophone was made of brass and it was heavy in the way that I couldn't describe until I held my first baby and let its head fall across my forearm so I could wash its hair. He borrowed his mother's chiffon headscarves so we could make the light change with a torch: an orange glow across the back of the set suggesting sunset; the crackling of the gramophone as we lowered the needle onto the record might have been rain or wind. Eventually we grew out of this game and the boy's father broke up the theatre and burned it. Everything was out of proportion: the theatre, the props, Lola, and the conversation I had years later with a sister about that game in the garage. How I hadn't understood that anyone could hurt me.

Later, he disappeared.
But first, a scene in his kitchen. A lamp throws shadows

onto the ceiling, spills light across a Formica tabletop. Two coffee mugs. The fine dark hairs on his wrist. His eyelashes. We carefully place everything not said into the small wooden box that once contained chess pieces. I stand up to leave. He watches me walk to the door.

JOHANNA EMENEY

Going into Winter

The autumn afternoons have crispened
yet still sprung and cycling
are the spiky lemon bottlebrushes.
Immersed in their fluted yellow,
bumble bees—some quite ordinary,
some potential queens—effervesce.
Lazily, lazily,
one might buzz the hair-trigger flanks
of horses quietly worrying hay
and a goat may startle at the spot
too close to her feed bowl
where one crawls like an old dark beetle
but it will be a few weeks before
dozens drop onto the shed's tin roof,
the sound of their unwinding bodies
a sick alarm.

Power of the Word

When she had pressed it flat
the milk-bottle top
was a silver disk.
She said it was a coin.

Odd to conceive now
that twixt-and-between self
believing and not believing
in Santa Claus;

trusting and not trusting
the brother on the upper bunk
when he said the sleigh
had passed the moon.

Yet seeing it. And the coin.
Easily crushed, dirt in its folds
but silver nevertheless.
A coin made by a word.

The Cleaners

The morning bustle of workers moved down the hallway from one meeting room to another.

'Susi,' Lavita hissed, wrinkles creasing her brown forehead. 'Put it in your bag before they see. Silly woman.'

'Relax.' Susi looked down the hall at the men and women in their neatly pressed suits. *They're too busy to see little old Susi and Lavita.* She shoved the Rolex into her pocket, as a woman in a white button-down shirt and dress pants strode past and narrowed her eyes. The watch caught on the edge of Susi's pocket and panic bubbled in her chest as she fumbled with it. The timepiece was worth more than an entire year's wages for a cleaner. Her fingers wrapped around it, safe inside the pocket. She grabbed a paper towel from the trolley, wiped the sudden sheen of sweat from her brow, and breathed through the adrenalin rush.

Head lowered, she walked softly, as if she could creep her way through the deception.

'Excuse me.' A clipped voice from behind.

Susi's body tensed.

'Hey, you. Wait a minute.'

A hand touched her shoulder and she gasped, her spirit leaping out of her skin in shock.

She turned slowly, heat rising beneath her cheeks.

'The coffee machine is empty, and I'm already late for my meeting. Can you refill it?'

'Of course, sir.'

Susi reset the coffee machine while Lavita wiped the remains of a salad from the bench. 'All done, sir.' Susi steeled herself then opened the dishwasher, wincing as a hot fist of steam flew at her face.

A tall man swaggered into the kitchenette wearing a three-piece suit and shoes as shiny as obsidian. Lavita leaned toward Susi and whispered in

Samoan. 'O lo`u tama lea, e tolu afe le pelaue o le tamaloā.' There he is. Mr Three-Thousand-Dollar Suit.

Susi stifled a giggle. 'Might need a new one when we're finished with him,' she whispered back.

The man reached past her, dumped a dirty cup onto her tray of clean dishes from the machine, then left.

A voice from the hall: 'Seen Tania's team, Andy?'

'Nope. Just came from the kitchen, nobody down there.'

Susi slammed the dishwasher shut with a clunk.

She leaned the vacuum cleaner hose against the fifth-floor window. The night sky was the black of the tithe-sucking priests back home. Silence hung over the office floor, interrupted only by the sound of water pattering on leaves as Lavita tended to the plants lining the wall.

'What is it today, Sus?' Lavita paused and stretched. 'Another watch? A phone?'

Susi smiled. 'The earrings. They're just so pretty.' She fingered the small dangling earrings in her pocket and giggled.

Lavita shrugged and carried on watering the plants. 'Any smiles today?'

'Just the one.'

'The guy with the rash on his face?'

Lavita nodded. 'The sad-looking ones are always the nicest.'

Paul stood on his toes, stretching his calves. The sooner he got the meeting over with, the sooner he could get to the gym.

Susi, the larger of the two Pacific Island cleaners, entered the meeting room late, and sat. 'Sorry, boss.' She smiled. 'Hard to get the kids to my sister this early at short notice.'

Paul raised his eyebrows. 'I know it's just you and the kids, Suzy, but it's important to be on time. Lanita was here early.' He looked at his watch and sighed. 'Some personal items have gone missing from the Hammerson offices.' *As if the thieving ingrates didn't already know.* 'Jewellery and electronics, mostly. We're investigating this at the moment, and should be finished doing so by the end of the week.' He looked straight at Susi and held back a grin. It was always so much fun watching them squirm. 'I just wanted to remind you we have a zero-tolerance policy when it comes to theft.' He hadn't wanted to remind them—would have preferred to catch them without warning—but HR had too much say.

Susi looked at the ground. 'Okay. Thanks, sir.'

Paul strode from the meeting room. Maybe he'd make the spin class after all.

Susi reached the lift as the doors started closing. Mister Three-Thousand-Dollar Suit was inside. He met her eyes, then looked back down at his phone.

Susi opened her mouth but the doors whooshed shut. *Arsehole.* That smile will be coming off soon. She caught the next lift down. Her uniform looked out of place in the elevator's mirrored wall, its dirty, worn fabric pressed against clean suits and blouses, but her black hair was oiled and immaculate like her grandmother's on Sunday. Susi's smile showed teeth as white as cowrie shells. She inched over so the expensive headphones in her bag didn't knock against the wall.

She rushed through the lobby, sat down on a bench in the smoking area and lifted the hood of her jacket against the wind.

'Only twenty minutes left for lunch,' Lavita tsked from the seat next to her.

Susi grunted in reply and took the leftover chop-suey from her bag. She shovelled the first cold spoonful down.

'Dunno why we're not allowed to use the kitchenette.' Lavita looked behind her at the lobby's giant screens showing clips of white people shaking hands. 'It's not like they're worried about the electricity bill for the microwave.'

'You *know* why,' Susi said in a stern voice. 'They don't want a couple of PIs sitting next to them. Might tell them how to do their jobs.' She cackled.

Lavita guffawed and nearly spat her lunch on the step.

Paul entered the room late and sat. He hadn't expected them to confess, but this would certainly speed the process along. 'Suzy. Lanita.' He smiled. 'Oh, and Alice. Morning.' He was surprised to see his manager there but could understand why they would want to tell her at the same time. Pull off the Band-aid in one go.

Susi raised her eyebrows. 'It's Soo-see, Paul. Ess, not zed. I know you haven't been working with us long, but it's important to use the correct name when addressing others.' Her steady voice was like a judge's addressing a courtroom.

Paul frowned in annoyance. He'd never heard the cleaning woman string so many words together.

Looking at the shiny watch on her wrist, Susi sighed. 'Lavita and I haven't been completely honest with you.'

Paul nodded, trying to keep the knowing smile from his face. *Here it comes.*

'We came in to do a job, on Alice's request.'

That wasn't entirely correct. Alice didn't have time to organise the cleaning staff personally. But Paul let her continue.

She handed him a sheet of paper. 'We wanted you here when we gave the findings to Alice.'

'Huh?'

The printout was a series of timestamped screen grabs from a video and showed a well-dressed man standing over someone's desk in the otherwise empty office. Paul squinted. Was that Andy from Accounts?

'We've been investigating the reported thefts in the Hammerson offices for some time now,' Susi said. 'Posing as cleaners gives a certain level of invisibility to PIs, sorry, Private Investigators ... in firms like your own.'

Paul repeated the words slowly in his head. *What?*

'In the images you can see one Andrew Saunders helping himself to a pair of earrings I planted on the desk,' Susi said. 'This is all the evidence Alice needs to begin disciplinary proceedings against the staff member. I'm sure you'll be involved in the process.'

Paul glanced up to find Susi staring at him. His cheeks flushed warm and he shifted in his seat.

'I've noted some of the ... challenges we found in carrying out the investigation, Paul. Your assumption that we committed the crime, without any evidence whatsoever, is concerning. There are lots of courses available on unconscious bias, Paul. I'm sure Alice will chat with you more about that.'

Paul looked at the paper trembling in his hands. He could feel his ears flushing with heat.

'Ia fa soifua, manuia lou malaga,' Susi said. 'Goodbye and good luck with the rest of the process, both of you.'

Susi strode out of the meeting room. The fluorescent light of the hall glinted on her gold Rolex. A gift from her mother after graduation, there was no need to hide it now.

NIGEL BROWN

Climate of Change

1. *Tipping Point*, 2018–19, acrylic with mixed media on canvas, 1350 x 800 mm.
2. *Sea Protect*, 2018–19, acrylic and beads on canvas, 1350 x 800 mm.
3. *Concrete History*, 2014, found objects, metal and acrylic on board,
   790 x 590 mm.
4. *Measure of Cook*, 2009–10, acrylic and found objects on board, 790 x 590 mm.
5. *Black Dog*, 2017, acrylic and wood on cut-out ply, 670 x 780 mm.
6. *Dogged by Raw Emotions*, 2018, acrylic and wood block on cut-out ply,
   730 x 610 mm.
7. *I Am Tower*, 2006–08, metal, cut-out ply, bone and acrylic on wood,
   670 x 440 x 440 mm.
8. *Black White Head*, 2005–06, found objects, metal, paint on wood,
   590 x 440 x 440 mm.

As a child I made toys out of builders' offcuts; my early creative efforts
included carving. Carving is a background thread to my woodcuts and
painting. I was raised on an orchard where my father practised for his bow
hunting with a crude mock-up deer and painted his arrows in our basement;
and I was read stories about wild places and remote tribes.

In the new millenium at Cosy Nook in Southland I was in a rural situation
with old fenceposts, farm debris and various influences from trips away
(working with Barry Brickell; visiting Evgeny Rastorguev in Russia; and
working with Richard Nunns). A book on the sculpture of Picasso gave further
impetus, as did African sculpture in the Eastern Southland Art Gallery.
Much time spent in op shops fossicking for Crown Lynn has led to random
elements in my work that have a recycling ethos, and reinforce new debate:
with all the talk now of sustainability and climate change combined with
identity issues there is much to give creativity strong impetus.

I have produced a good deal of work on Captain Cook, looking at him both
historically and pulled into the contemporary world. I'm not a conventional
memorialiser and find more pleasure in doubt, contradiction and questioning.

—Nigel Brown

CLIMATE OF CHANGE

TIPPING POINT

NIGEL BROWN 2011-2012

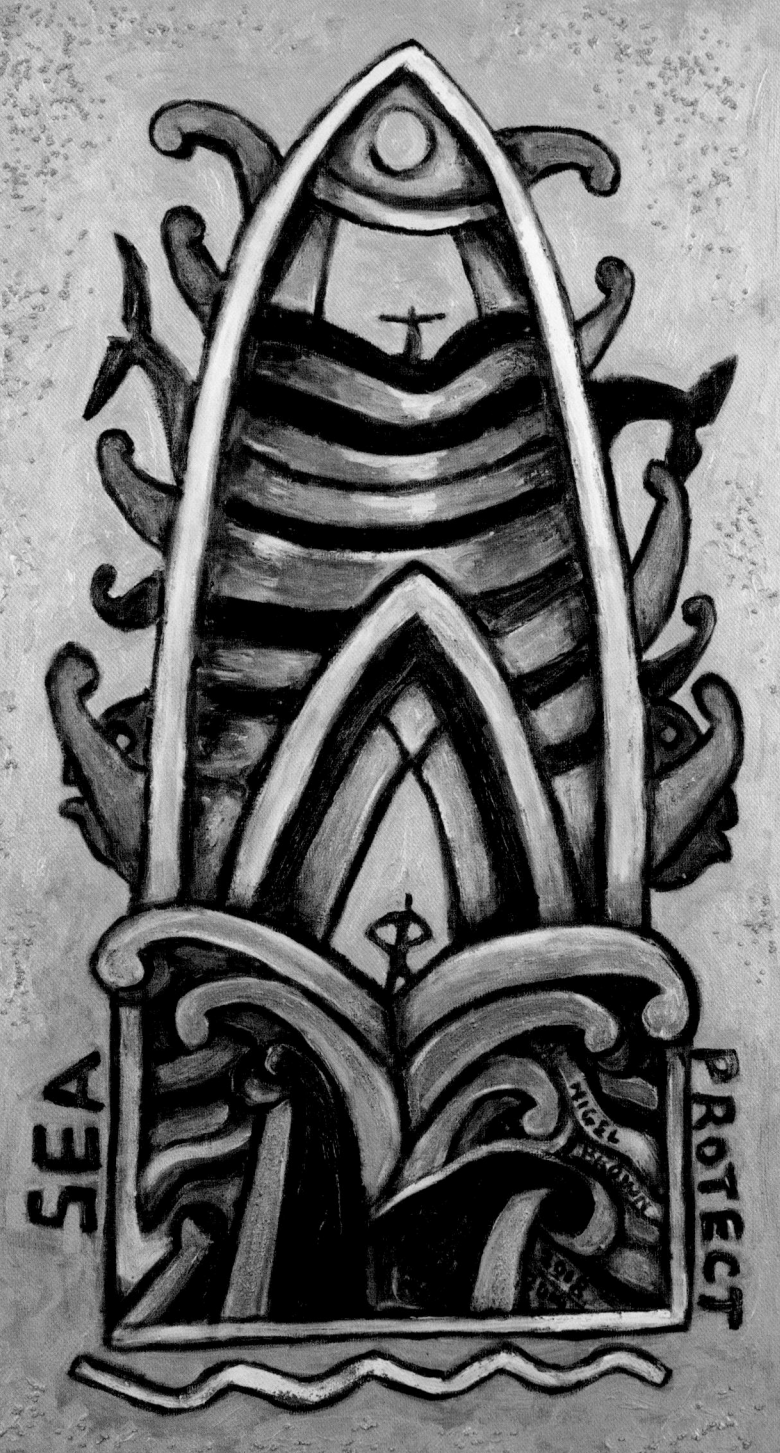

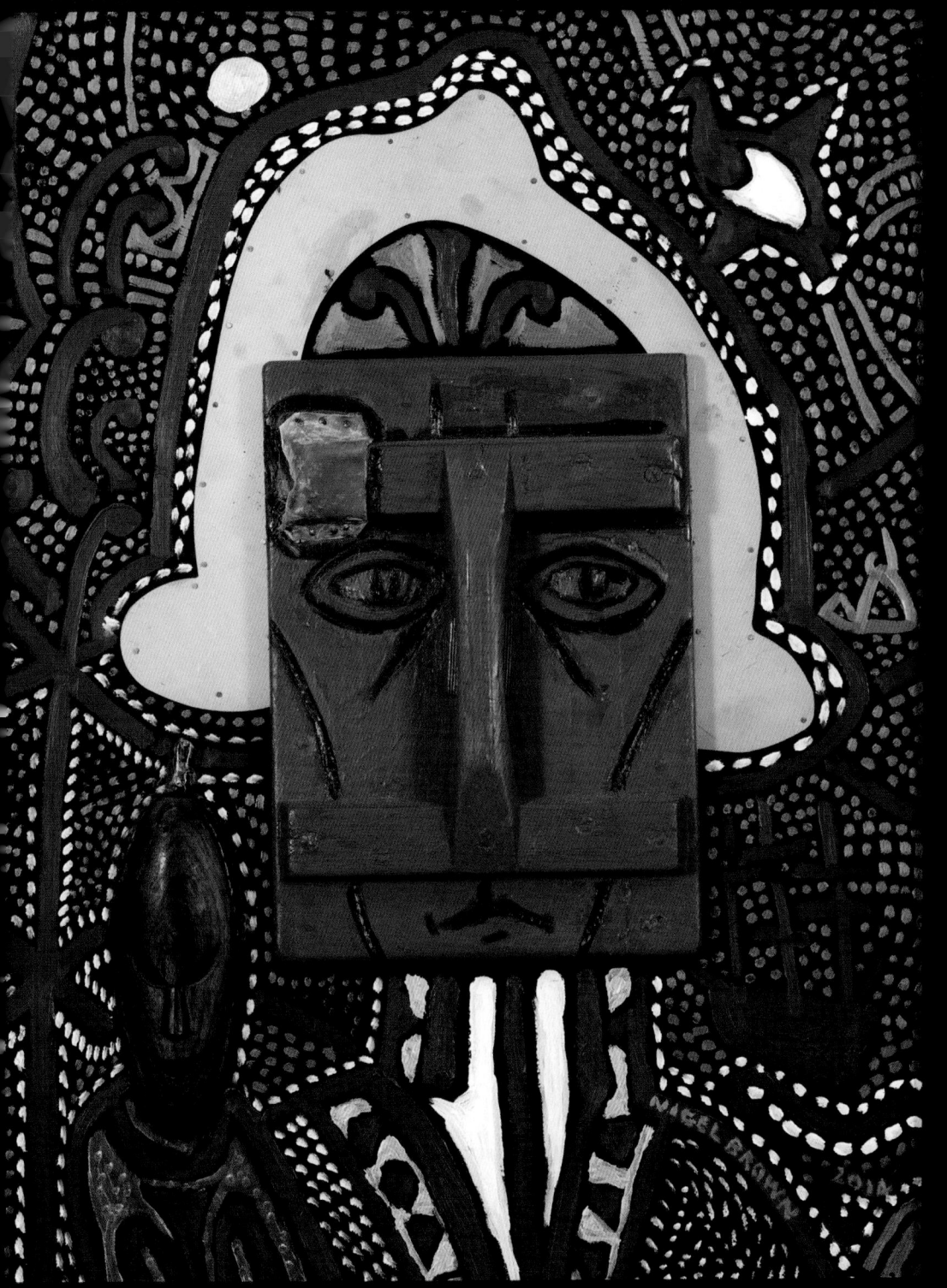

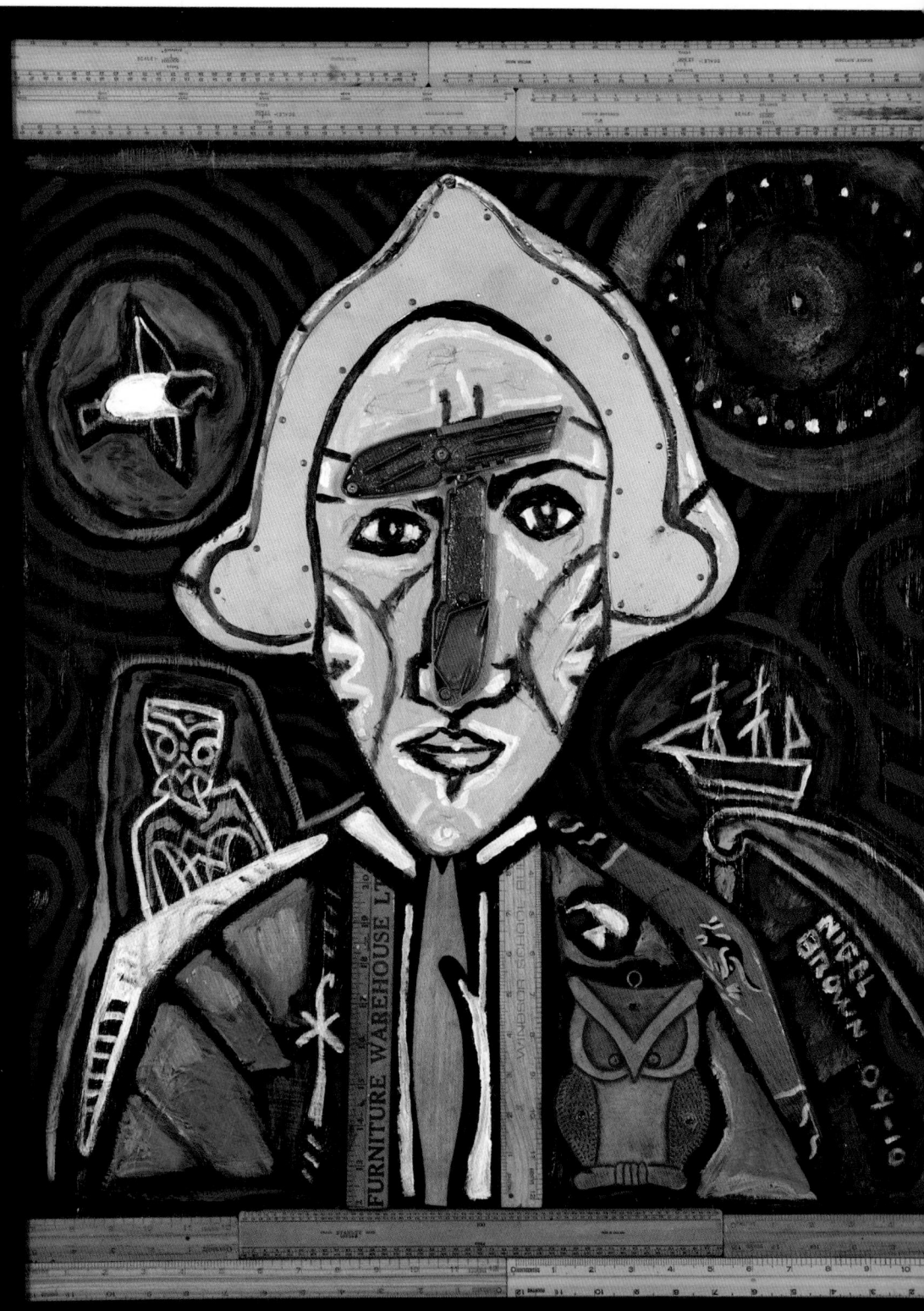

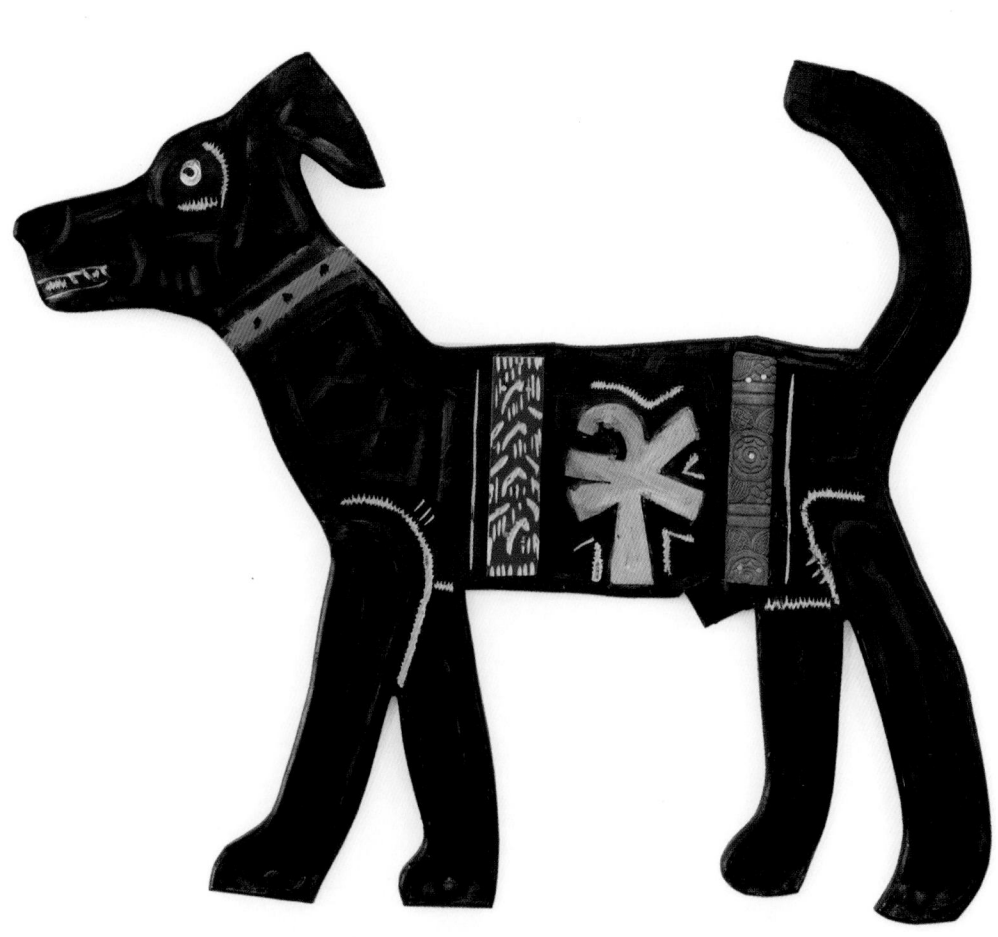

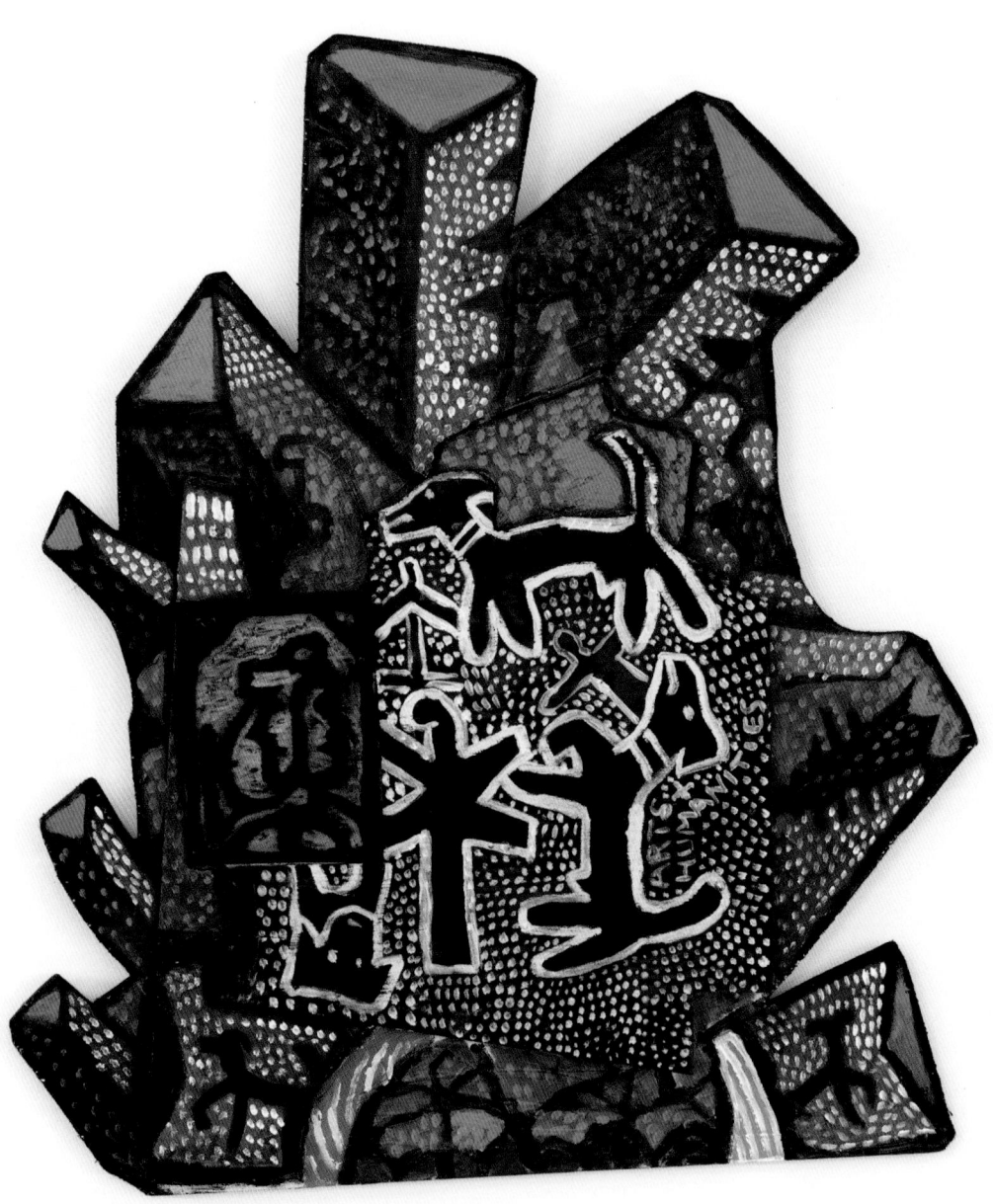

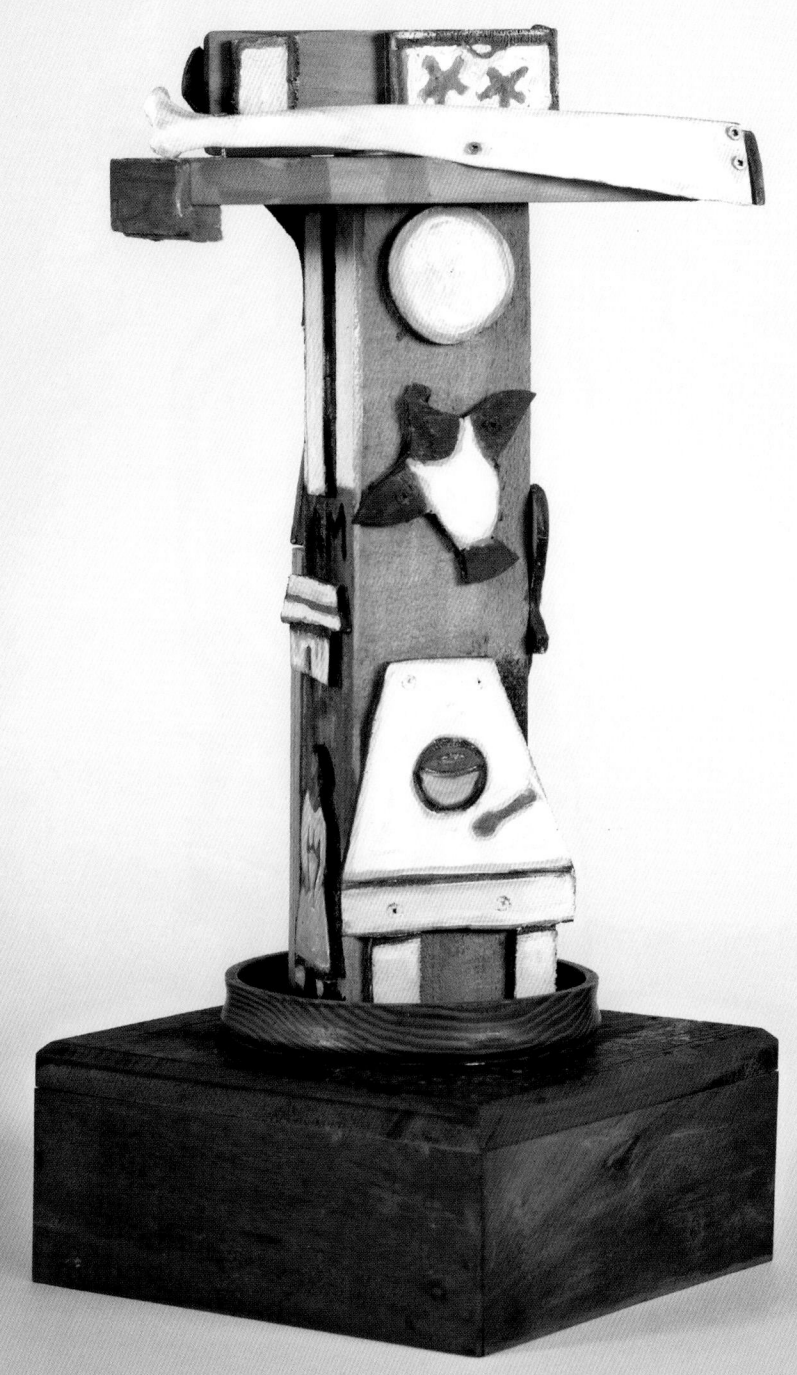

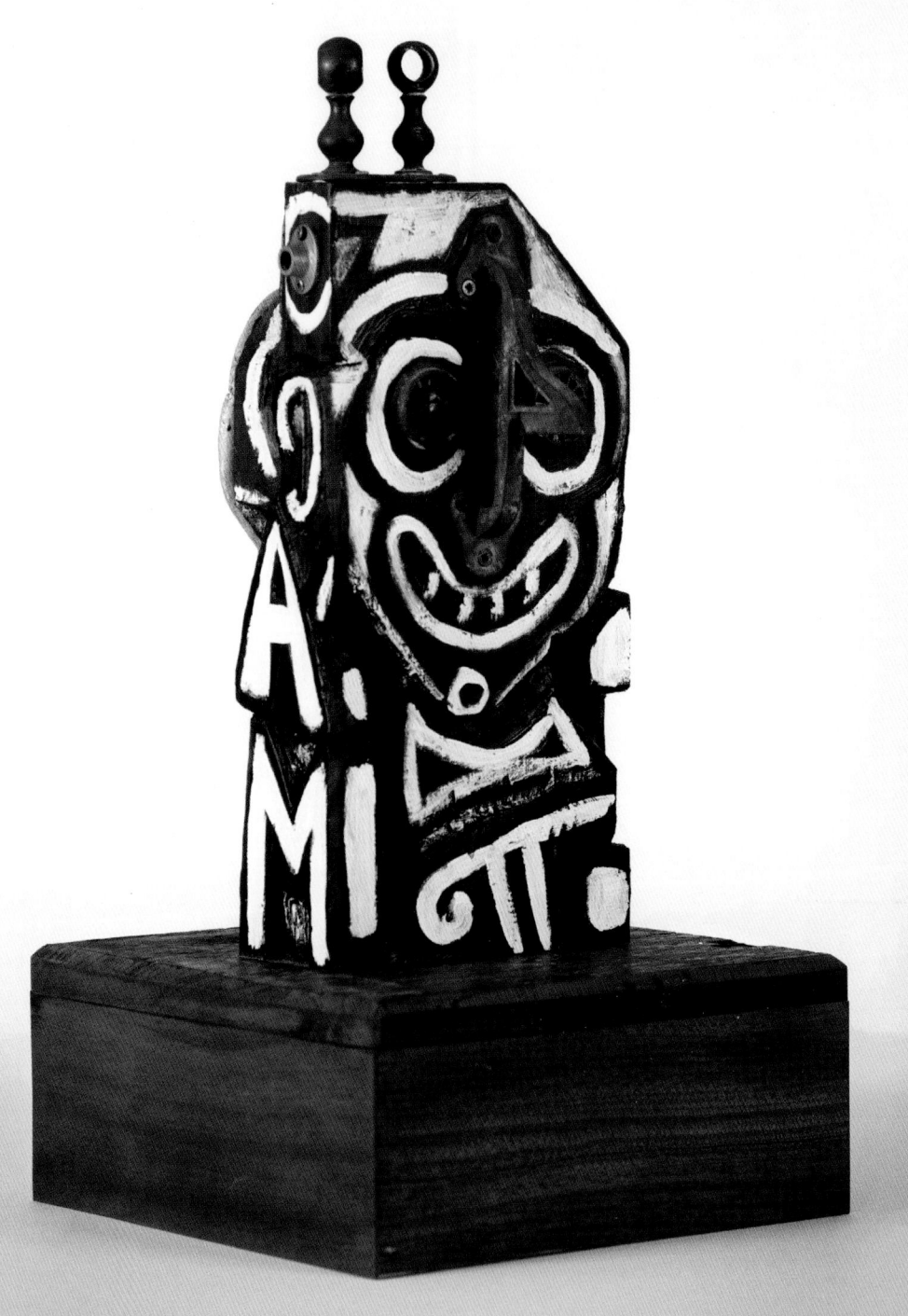

Bloody Awful

The last words my father said to me were 'bloody awful'
when I asked how are you Dad I had never heard him
say such a negative thing about himself except when
he cried as he told me about his mate at the children's
home who hanged himself after he was interfered with
by a priest who was supposed to be his protector it was
bloody awful and there he was my father his last few hours
on earth staunch again as he always was and me leaving
both of us knowing we would probably never see each
other again and I holding his hand and searching his eyes
which were the same blue as his pyjamas and loving him
without words and he knew and he squeezed my hand
before I left and watched me go and it was bloody awful

ANNA KATE BLAIR

Marguerite Duras at the Tepid Baths

I am asked, soon after I start swimming regularly, what it is that I think about while I swim. I think, at first, of numbers. I count the strokes, the laps, and hold each number in my mind until I touch the end of the pool and take another. I think, after that, about my mother, who swam almost every day in the years before she died; I think, still, of numbers, of how old she was when she died, how old I am now, the digits of the day of the month on which she died. It seems, now, uncomfortably easy to move from twenty-seven laps to thirty-two, from thirty-two to forty; it seems that each stroke is bringing me closer to an impossible number, to a number that gestures toward death. I think of how the number of laps my mother swam each day, when I was a child, seemed mythical, a grand feat of endurance, something to brag about to the other children at school, and I think of the notebook in which she detailed her cancer treatment, of the recurrence of that word on every page: *swam*.

I think, as I swim, of sentences I could write that I just can't seem to keep, that vanish as the numbers come, so that I feel forced to choose between more laps and my notebook in the locker. It begins with description, with the jewels that sparkle atop the water, with the difficulty of getting that sparkling, fluttering surface, that refusal of flatness, into prose or, at least, not clichéd prose. It's so common to write that these dashes of light are *like diamonds*, but they still look like it, feel like it.

I am not really a swimmer. I like activities that I can record, but I must secure my notebook, my phone and my glasses in a locker. I have chosen to swim because I am, in Auckland, close to my favourite public pool, the Tepid Baths, where the tiled walls are decorated with interwar photographs and ferns still hang in baskets above the water. It is an aesthetic decision; I wish to swim because I like the space. I wonder, also, if I could love swimming as my mother loved swimming (though I wonder, too, if she loved it). I am surprised to find that I enjoy swimming; I walk to the Tepid Baths again the next day and then the next day and then my partner breaks up with me, after five years, and suddenly I can do almost nothing but swim.

On Instagram, I find a photograph of Marguerite Duras, taken in a photobooth in the 1940s. Her hair is parted and brushed upward, backward, into messy buns on either side of her head. Behind her ear, at her neck, a strand extends outward, loose. She has a large, pale forehead; she wears dark lipstick and does not smile, does not frown. She looks down toward the left corner of the image, such that her eyelids are large, voluptuous, and her eyelashes form a fringe over her eyes, barely open. She wears a striped jacket over a high-necked blouse.

She looks, in the photograph, so satisfied. She presents herself to the camera in such a straightforward way, as one does in a photo booth, and yet, with those eyelids she is never available, always elsewhere. She appears, even before the camera, in complete control.

In the next lane a woman and a girl bounce up and down, playing in the water, swimming together. The girl is in a purple swimsuit, bright against the chlorinated water; her bent legs dance in and out of the frame made by my goggles. She seems about ten, I think. She is a girl on the precipice at which I ceased to have a mother. I feel like crying sometimes when I see young girls with women in their late thirties, but it is easy, in the pool, to move away, to spread my hand out ahead of me in the water, to consider my nails, dashes of red made purple underwater.

In the pool I am forced into myself because I can't see hard outlines, only light and colour. I must squint at the signs, a metre away, to determine which lane is marked SLOW. Everything is smudged, out of focus. There is an underwater sensation to everything, even above the water; it's all echoes, no present tense, noumenal time, or no time, maybe. I don't have a watch or phone; I can't see the clock on the wall without my glasses. It is easy, here, to lose myself, which is what I want, I suppose.

I replay events as I swim. He sent a text message to break up with me, as if it were almost nothing. I begged him to call me, to talk to me, and he eventually gave in but wouldn't answer my questions. I cried and he hung up on me. He sent me the telephone number of a suicide hotline, told me to call them instead. He told me, a week later, in another text message, that my sadness had caused him to see me in a bad light, that my sadness was manipulative and unreasonable.

I conjure explanations, refine them with each stroke. He left me because he met somebody else, I suppose, somebody with an American passport, somebody less complicated by depression and ambition. I have seen, on the internet, that he introduced her to his parents less than two weeks after he broke up with me. It's clear, in some ways, but I still can't understand it.

I feel, sometimes, a physical fury while swimming; I want, with each stroke, to make a case for why my anger is justified. I find myself addressing my sentences to my former partner, thinking in the second person. There is a rawness to you; it's rarely elegant. I take this anger, which I have never felt before, out on the surface of the pool. I swim to get away from the ugliness of my feelings, but I am swimming in a pool, turning and tacking, going nowhere, always in the same confined space, in the same moment, tracing the same conversation, unable to move forward.

I begin to think, as I swim, about Marguerite Duras; also about the photographs from the 1940s, about the quality of her prose, which is at once fragmentary and liquid. I envy her for the ways in which she seems alive to desire, effortlessly, instinctively. She writes, often, of what it is to live in a body, to be governed by that. I wonder if my partner broke up with me because I lacked this effortlessness, because I did not know who or what I wanted, because I told him I felt lost. *You communicate too much*, he said, or typed, when I kept asking for a reason.

It could have been mutual. If he'd said: *we're more like friends, anyway, aren't we?* I would have said: *yes*.

I read about women who learn to inhabit their bodies through running, through dancing, through aerial hoop. I find, though, that I am telling my body what to do, never listening to it, being guided by it. I am hoping, as I swim, that I might learn to follow my body, to see it as myself.

This misery over a breakup is, though, another form of grieving. I was too young, when my mother died, to grieve directly; I latch on, as an adult, to situations in which I might replay that death. I think of Hiroshima, Mon Amour, Marguerite Duras's movie, in which the desire to process one's individual sorrow takes on grand proportions, subsumes history. I, too, have focused on communal sorrows, looked at the trauma of history instead of my own childhood. I cry over extinct birds, over the demolition of Robin Hood Gardens, over French colonisation, the Aids crisis, the death of Lou Reed. Each is an excuse for sadness, an outlet. It seems voyeuristic, juvenile; I can't, as Sylvia Plath did, equate my own suffering with the Holocaust, but I understand the impulse, guard against it. I think of Hiroshima, Mon Amour as the limit, balancing danger with self-awareness.

It isn't one rejection, but every loss before it surging forward, swirling around me. I've thought, each time I've been unwanted, that I've never felt worse, never been sadder. I'm sure that's not true, I'm told, others assuming that each loss is compartmentalised, not cumulative. I feel a fresh reminder of the ways in which my mother's death will always be ongoing, of the ways in which my relationships are shaped by it. I can only watch as loss repeats itself.

I wonder, sometimes, if I am drawn to female writers because I do not have a mother, because I am trying to create my own lineage, and yet a good writer is never a good parent to the reader. There is often, for me, an element of desire; I fall in love with language. It is the only real intimacy I have with older women, I suppose; I read the words that they wrote, realise that they were often as lost as me. I find, in them, phrases for the uncertainty that haunts the blank spaces of my mother's notebook, which is not a diary but a set of lists, of medications taken and foods eaten, of daily habits. Swam.

In The Lover, Marguerite Duras writes of desire as something forceful, predetermined: all is swept away in the torrent, in the force of desire. Duras writes as she appears in the photograph, with clarity and absence. She writes of a narrator with a face that reveals her future, *a face of pleasure* that shows sexual readiness and attracts others. I think of her eyelids in the photo booth, of my instant infatuation with that image. If our faces and bodies communicate to others, instinctively, I fear that mine offers only endings, an intimation of loss.

'It is a bit pointless, isn't it?' I said once to my psychoanalyst about sex, and he laughed.

There are so many things that are pointless, though: sex; swimming; writing; life.

There are great spaces where you think there used to be someone, but it's not true, wrote Marguerite Duras. *There was no one.*
    I think of the swimming pool, emptied each night, as it fills with water in the early morning, becomes again a space in which to move, to float, to linger.

I aspire to swimming as a means of release. I am trying to leave my thoughts in the pool, to allow myself to forget or fail to record some things. I wonder if my words, unspoken underwater, might drain away after I leave. I am trying to see the pool as a place where voices are muffled by water, where sounds and sensations do not necessarily become sentences. At the end of the lane, encouraging somebody else to swim ahead of me, I gesture instead of speaking. I am surrounded by the lapping sounds of water draining at the pool edge, by the chopping of swift arms in the fast lane, though high-pitched squeals detached from bodies, echoing off the roof, above the water, have a sort of melody too.
    I am lying by omission, though, by implication. I am compressing hours of swimming, clumsily and desperately, into an essay, presenting only one side of a breakup, presenting grief as something that I might understand. I am trying to let go, to inhabit my body, and yet I have not mentioned, until now, that I have started bringing a notebook to the pool, leaving it with a pen beside my towel at the water's edge, rather than in my locker. It would be more truthful, perhaps, to say that I am only half-heartedly letting go, that I am watching myself as I do so, that I hope that when I finish this piece, I might swim without the notebook, might write only: *swam.*

The shearer

arrives in a dented Datsun,
ties the portable unit to a post
with electric blue baling twine,
bundles the ewe against her crotch.

The wool is grey and stuck with docks
but when she shears it falls away
like taking off a robe. Underneath
is cream and gilded in sun looks gold.

Her arms, varnished with lanolin,
shine as under lights. The ewe's skin
is pink and flushed. Graceful
limbs and torsos entwine

until the lulling background buzz
of the handpiece ends. She unbends
as from a bow, pitches the gear
in the car like sacks of wheat,

drives across the ruts, the only
remembrance of their fleeting dance
the golden fleece, froth of lace
and tulle, bobbing on the back seat.

JANET NEWMAN

HMS *Orpheus*

No songs. Just the hard vault of sand.
Against that bank the hull locks,
crew climb rigging, twine around knots.
Waves do the rest, land

blows at spars, snap wood to bits.
Limbs break when the jibstay drops.
The main mast dives past the mizzentop.
Sloshed canvas sails are cold bassinets.

I, who chart the harbour's past, derive
from one fished from the undertow,
a wet-faced boy, gelid, alive,
paddled to shore, gasping. I throw

myself to the grabbing foam,
wrangle a mongrel wave, ride it home.

*My great-grandfather, ordinary seaman Henry Newman, was 17 years
old when he survived the Orpheus shipwreck at the entrance to Manukau
Harbour in 1863, which drowned 189 crew. Henry was presumed drowned
and his sister, born later that year in the Channel Island of Jersey, was named
Orpheus.*

LISSA MOORE

The Green Sweater

In Hallenstein's the assistant with the brown eyes
tells me my son can come by any time and change

the sweater I am holding up to the fluorescent lights
but I say no—thank you—grateful she can't see him

still lying on the mattress on the floor in the darkened
room, so I just hold the sweater up again to be sure.

This colour. This deep green of moss I am already falling
in love with, that I already need close by me, to touch, almost

as soft as my dog's head under my hand. All those near-
invisible stitches made by someone I will never meet

in a country where I have never been. There is no sweater
in the world warm enough to carry back to him. I don't know

where to look or who to ask for such a thing in this strange city, if
such a thing exists. But I pay the lady, take the bag, hold it close

and walk back out onto the street where I wait as if waiting for a sign
and the trucks go by and the buses, the cars and all the people,

the people, like a grey river, with nowhere to cross.

Spring

There are several melon flowers growing on the balcony. I don't know where they came from. I have no memory of planting melon seeds. I had to go to the internet to ask for advice. It told me that if I ever wanted a melon it was likely I would have to hand-pollinate due to the problem of the bees ever finding my balcony. Even though they fly, they avoid heights. The female flower is only open for one day so you have to work quickly, if possible first thing in the morning between seven and nine. You can either pluck off the male flower and directly rub him up and down on the female or you can take a paintbrush and brush the male stamen with it and then paint the pollen onto the female. By the end of the day both flowers will have wilted and will eventually fall off. It was not a nice way to read one's own biography and I had to shut the computer for a while and rest before deciding what to do next.

ALBERT WENDT

In the Garden Again

The dank smell of upturned spring earth continues seeping into our house
Since nine the two gardeners have been mowing   weeding   turning
over the garden beds and planting the flowers and vegetables
Reina brought back from the garden shop

For over a week I'd not felt well so yesterday I saw my doctor
who prescribed antibiotics for my infected throat
and exercises for my sore right shoulder and tingling arm and fingers
In our frank conversation and his caring examination the huddled anxiety
eased out of my centre and I agreed to see my psychologist

I go onto the back deck of our house and stand under the pergola
at the railing that is lined with pot plants of flowers   herbs and chillies
in sun-glittering reds   yellows   blues and violets that catch and lift
my breath to embrace our garden in its passionate fragrance

The gardeners glance up at me smile   wave and then continue
clipping the back hedge   their feet planted in the black soil
I can't see Reina and Manoa anywhere: their absence is worrying
for always they are at the centre of our garden and my need for
symmetry and completeness in spring's wild hunger for expression

MIRIAMA GEMMELL

The Difference between Midnight and Dawn

the painter has been in my hallway again
a few flecks each day
apostrophes becoming parasols and poppies
grace saves us all

by night the artery is a dark swamp of teeth
alligator plastic, creaking bones
under the blinding glare
my fist beats the walls

ONE TWO   THREE
the mosquitos drag their entrails behind them
dramatic little toreadors

Family Tree

1.1.1 cousin wants the whakapapa
1.1.2 cousin played reps back in the day
1.1.3 cousin bringing the leftovers
1.2.1 cousin baby four on the way

1.2.2 cousin gone to the tangi
1.2.3 cousin overtime pretty busy
1.2.4 cousin one more month of curfew
1.2.5 cousin moving back to brizzie

1.3.1 cousin trying to learn the reo
1.4.1 cousin raffle for the touch trip
1.4.2 cousin got the korowai
1.4.3 cousin always had a lip

1.5.1 cousin tryna straighten out
1.5.2 cousin makes a mean fry
1.7.1 cousin too shame to do your song
1.7.2 cousin got a DUI

1.7.3 cousin had another miscarriage
1.8.1 cousin separated now
1.8.2 cousin wants to work the land
1.9.1 cousin just doesn't know how

1.9.2 cousin pretty into church
1.9.3 cousin bringing extra mince
1.9.4 cousin knows who broke in
1.9.5 cousin not been quite right since

1.10.1 cousin is the spit of nan
1.10.2 cousin kinda got the blues
1.10.3 cousin owes a bit of money
1.11.1 cousin tidied up the shoes

1.11.2 cousin never leaves the house
1.11.3 cousin is a skinny miss
1.12.1 cousin being a bloody nuisance
1.12.2 cousin come give us a kiss

SAM KEENAN

Better Graces

This story is the inaugural winner of the Sargeson Prize, New Zealand's richest short story prize, named for celebrated New Zealand writer Frank Sargeson and sponsored by the University of Waikato. This year's judge was Catherine Chidgey.

We like Miss Honour, even when she says 'Shhhhhh!', even when she hisses it over us like a punctured tyre that's on its way to deflating. We cross our arms high. We hide the holes in our pinafore frocks. We conceal our mothers' imperfect arranging of our hair, how it falls all spidery and disreputable. Dis-rep-u-ta-ble. Sound out each syllable so you know how to spell. It is appalling to be thought of as disreputable.

'You cannot be a good person without effort,' says Miss Honour after roll call, her starched collar peeking whitely from her dress. Concentrate all your thinking on being good or you won't do it properly. Sound it out. Con-cen-trate. You might be like the false people, all handsome and clean-like, smooth-saying 'Good morning children' with a Scottish burr. You might kiss hands all charming, all smiling, while Mrs Mudge spits 'Tssk!'

Miss Honour stands over us while we do our handwriting, and we write sentences about how to be good. We use the words 'nice' and 'kind' not knowing if Miss Honour's billowy sighs are because of our handwriting or the uncomplicated words contained within it. We sit blankly with our failings, whatever they might be—we shoo them away like the roaming hens, fat, feathery and annoying, and in the way of Right.

'Right is the proper way,' says Miss Honour. Right is the only thing that will save us. Miss Honour smiles at the boys that seem the Right ones, they of the pressed shirts and side-parts and fluttery black lashes. But how quickly the world turns to terrible when they are disappointing.

Jacob walks to Miss Honour's desk and presents his handwriting. He flicks his cowlick appealingly. Miss Honour takes his slate and pores over it in silence. She pores over it like scripture—difficult to decipher and full of unwelcome news.

'Did you take *care* when you wrote this, Jacob?' Miss Honour asks.

Jacob looks down himself at his neat socks and perfectly tied shoes. He feels our eyes on his back like burning holes as he is cast adrift in the sea of Miss Honour's question.

'If I asked you what percentage of care you took when you wrote this, Jacob, what would that percentage be?'

'Arrrr, ummm,' says Jacob, filling the air with sounds that don't say anything.

Another silence drifts across the classroom, and then Jacob says, 'I think I did take about 83 percent of care.'

Miss Honour does her stare, the one that's a flame against your face. 'Only 83 percent of care?'

Jacob looks down at the floorboards.

'What has happened to that 17 percent? Where did it go, Jacob?'

Jacob says nothing.

'Did you spend it on some other teacher, Jacob?' Miss Honour's voice deepens. 'I thought I was your loveliest teacher? Look at me, Jacob. I am *very* sad.'

We see the corners of Jacob's mouth turn downward. We watch him try to hold in his own sad, but it spills from his edges like a cloth used to mop up far too much water.

Miss Honour ups her voice so it's close to a shout and carries on all stern, 'Don't you *like* me enough to take care, Jacob? Don't you think I am *good* enough?'

Jacob's face scrunches up tight. He snatches his slate, sprints to his seat and hides his face in his shirt. Miss Honour looks well satisfied, like she is the queen of spiders and Jacob is one of her sickly flies. She throws us girls a look as if we are co-conspirators.

'We can't blame the *boys* for everything, now, can we?' she asks in a loud whisper, like it's a special secret to be let in on. 'Whose fault is it if we don't look after ourselves? It really *must* be my doing if I am not Jacob's loveliest teacher.' She directs us to look at the boys while she continues. 'Surely it's a woman's fault if she does not remain desirable. We can't blame the men who appear to love us and flatter us, then settle on finding us a bore.'

We nod with false knowing.

'Men, boys. They seem so kindly, but consider their misleadingness, girls, the way they lift their hats as if you might be special, how they act as if they have respect.' She turns to the boys and says 'RES-PECT.' Then we sit in silence until the bell sounds.

At interval, we watch Miss Honour in the resource room. We watch her as she watches Mr Palmer in the playground. There he is consoling the awkward relief teacher, draping his warm arm around her, looking her in the eye when she's speaking. His shirt is beautifully pinstriped. See him squeeze her hand as she sobs, while around them the wind lifts and scatters the leaves from the oaks and sends shivers through the flax. It catches Mr Palmer's jacket and the relief teacher's thinned-from-screaming hair as they sit together on the playground bench. The field behind them stretches up the hill to nowhere where evergreens sprawl around the creeks—the high place Miss Honour calls 'wretched' because there is just no room for roses with the pungas fanning their dark below the canopy, preventing the sunlight from getting in.

'Some of us must live in the dark,' says Miss Honour in morning science. 'There have to be those who are *unfortunate*, or the word *fortunate* would not exist.' She teaches us to hear loneliness in the throats of birds, and how the sound in the valley is a deep hollow you can feel.

We stay away from the boys at lunchtime. We must do as we are told or the world will chew us up and spit us out and into the poor people's houses to sit with babies and sick. We see their houses from the school's front gate. We see old papers blow into their front door steps which remain unswept. Miss Honour asks us to consider the very many ways there are to fail, what with babies and husbands, and no babies and no husbands. Two boys yell to us 'Come and play tag', but tag could be a terrible reckoning. It could lead you on to the path of Wrong, which is like a snow-covered mountain that is steep and slippery and ends with you falling on your face.

'We cannot play tag,' we say. We don't raise our voices, because that's only for adults talking to children. There is no screaming between Right adults, or from children on the side of Right.

In afternoon arithmetic, Mr Palmer's face peers around the doorframe.

'All right for assembly?' he asks, and Miss Honour swallows as if she is drinking an ocean and murmurs 'yes' in what seems like just the wrong tone.

'Got the certificates?' asks Mr Palmer, and Miss Honour lets out an unnatural-sounding 'yes'.

'See you soon,' he says, and Miss Honour husks an almost inaudible 'yes', and red ups her face like she's been too much in the sun. When Mr Palmer goes, she shakes her head and says things to herself. She lets out noises like the hushed whispers she thwacks us girls for.

'Girls must have better graces,' says Miss Honour in afternoon social studies. We listen as she tells us how to become ladies. Don't be like her. Don't be humiliated. Hu-mi-li-a-ted. Be high and silent. Don't spill your feelings so. If you feel sad and lovesick, pour your achiness into the playground creek, climb up away from it into the reaches of the biggest evergreen. Wait for the swollen berries to turn the colour of burning lanterns and your silly-girl feelings won't be painful as much. Girls are born to have painful feelings. They were made to bear the weight of the world. Consider the word 'career' before you embark on it. Think about how it might make you unlovely.

Mr Palmer passes by the room again and asks briskly, 'Do you have any matters of discipline?'

Miss Honour shakes her head and Mr Palmer offers no words in return. He walks away, and Miss Honour's straightness collapses a little.

After the afternoon break our clothes are damp. Miss Honour sees the discolouration on our skirts and faces. 'Don't you go getting them creek fishes,' she says, and we laugh because we know they aren't fishes, only Michael (not his real name) tries to explain. Michael (not his real name) does not realise when he has stepped off one tongue and onto another, and the word with its vowel sounds ups the room with magic, lights the shadows, brings a flicker to Miss Honour's eye as he says, 'They are kōura.'

We set about gasping at the forbiddenness, at the sight of a word meant to be kept in dark rooms being shaken out in the light of day. We hold our breath inwards to will away the sound, but it lingers like drifting particles, like dandelion seeds all soft and open, hanging in the air.

Miss Honour knows good so well. She knows it as she marches Michael (not his real name) off to Mr Palmer for justice. Justice is about Right and Wrong. We must learn from our punishments and mistakes; they are manifestations of Wrong. We must better ourselves. We can't sit and cry and moan and pine. We must make new plans and resolve never to be on the side of Wrong again.

Miss Honour strides so handsomely. The thick fabric of her dress grazes the naked arm of Michael (not his real name) as she leads him to the office. He hides his upsetness, but we see it plain as a bee struggling at a window looking all hopeless and desperate onto the world outside.

At afternoon assembly, Michael (not his real name) is sat at the front. His various sins are read: 'Did speak on the school grounds a language that is forbidden. Did fail to apologise immediately after.' Mr Palmer readies his whip. We try to remain calm and serene, because the punishment punishes the judge more than the criminal. It is hard for good people to rightly enforce the rules, but rules are there for reasons, and it would be no good to let bad deeds go unpunished. What would the world be like then? Pain can save us, says Miss Honour, like when she let her heart be ripped out all ripe and red. How could she have been so stupid? We need to punish ourselves. We need to punish others to stop them from being stupid again. We must save them from her humiliation. Hu-mi-li-a-tion.

Outside the hall, a soft wind brushes across the fields, and when the whip strikes, it's as if the wind catches Michael (not his real name) in its grip. He sucks inwards and inwards and his face is full of fright, only Mr Palmer doesn't notice and whips him again. Now the wind has Michael (not his real name) good and proper, and carries his breath away with it. The breath is the soul, Miss Honour told us in religious studies, and sure enough the wind takes the soul of Michael (not his real name) to wherever it is the wind takes things.

When Mr Palmer sees him go all limp like a river eel, his face becomes wide-eyed and huge, and Miss Honour catches this wide-eyed hugeness. She plays with her hands; she moves her head slowly. 'Come children,' she says, and leads us from the hall. We follow her to where she takes us, which is away and away from our classroom and the school hall and the schoolyard. We follow her to our town's highest field, all blank and open. And suddenly all the world is full of breath, as if it had been whipped out of Michael (not his real name) and scattered among the grasses, where it crawls through the green and brown blades like a scurrying thing until it runs completely out of sight.

DINAH HAWKEN

Caselberg Trust International Poetry Prize 2019 Judge's Report

To move from 200 poems through a longlist to a shortlist I began to develop a checklist. I began to see more clearly what—in my mind—makes an attractive, sustainable poem. But, like all poetry readers, I know I have subjective leanings and I'd like to make some of them clear.

I warm to a poem that makes an impact emotionally as well as an impact of ideas and description. I like poems that, in my serious mind, 'really matter' in this unsettled world. I'm partial to poems that show a love of the natural world because, even with us in it, our landscape continues to be inspiring and generative. (I was glad to meet many poems among the entries that began in the landscape and expressed concerns about climate change.) I'm also interested in the psychological understanding some poems offer—as insight, fellow feeling or consolation. I think now of this poem from the shortlist:

It hasn't taken long
to feel tired of the world.
The crunch of snow
now given way to the
sharp edge of words.

Trying to hold them,
my will to melt them.
To hand them back
magnanimous
softer than they came.

Economy and insight can make a strong poem. And sometimes a single line makes a particular personal impact, as in this one: 'But up they go, the stems, or went, or will.' That line will stay with me as a reminder and a consolation for a long time.

To return to the checklist, the first characteristic of a good poem must surely be a genuine love of language—in the many ways it can show itself. As Jane Hirshfield writes: 'Every good poem begins in language awake to its own connections—language that hears itself and what is around it ...' Most of the poems that missed my longlist were missing such awareness. Some were moving and valuable as individual responses to a situation, but without an obvious love of language, its infinite sounds and possibilities, the poet is like an artist who doesn't care much about her materials. Language in a poem doesn't need to be flamboyant or 'poetic'. A poem can be 'language-awake' with the choice of a single surprising adjective, as in this poem from the shortlist (possibly written by a young person) about a cat:

> I sometimes wonder
> where do you go Henry
> when the people all leave
> and you are all alone
> with that undecided smile.

The second essential characteristic is distinctiveness. I asked of each poem: have I heard you, or a poem like you, too often before? Originality and imagination, also on my list, differ I think from a distinctive voice in a poem. The ability to be original and/or imaginative seems an innate creative quality, difficult to cultivate, perhaps akin to talent? I know I wish I had more of it.

There is a process in the making of a poem I am calling sensitive observation: sensitivity to the experience, place, words that initiate a poem; as well as sensitivity during the writing where more discoveries are made. The outer and inner perceptions intertwine. Attentiveness to both is central to a good poem and seems to produce a natural subtlety.

The shortlisted poems had very little awkwardness in their movements from line to line, and they had an ear for rhythm—a rhythm that complemented the tone and feeling of the poem.

Even in the poems I've chosen I can sometimes hear a need for more careful crafting and greater clarity. I didn't understand a number of them, and I tried to distinguish lack of clarity from plain difficulty—when the poet knows more than you do and you need the internet and dictionary! Clarity is tricky when you also value mystery, drama and surprise in a poem, which I do, but clarity makes a strong essential connection with the reader.

So measuring the poems against my checklist—looking for love of language, distinctiveness, imagination, sensitive observation, musicality, craft, surprise, clarity and a respect for the reader—edged me toward my final, often difficult, decisions.

First prize goes to 'The Social Media Cat Got Their Tongues' by **Gail Ingram**; and second prize to 'The Fungibility of Thought' by **Derek Schulz**. These two poems appear on the following pages. There are five highly commended entries: 'Dog' by **Mary Macpherson**; 'R Channels David Attenborough' by **Mary Macpherson**; 'Somebody Killed the Cat' by **Emer Lyons**; 'Second Language' by **Ruby Solly**; and 'Catch and Release' by **Alan Roddick**. All these poems are published on the Caselberg Trust's website.

GAIL INGRAM

The Social Media Cat Got Their Tongues

Crying help while the cat
slipped around their legs, her tail
wrapping and coiling them
as she went. They longed to run
their fingers through the soft
white fur. Everybody
reached for the cat, thinking of
a Russian princess, and she purred
a soft rumble like tyres over gravel.
The people mistook the pinpricks
under their skin for blood
shot through with royalty. For it was
a striking cat
with a very long tail coiled
around the crowd, sending
the people toppling.

DEREK SCHULZ

The Fungibility of Thought

So what about the post-human era? —Martin Rees

Let's go deeper. We're retroventing
the human race right now, trans-
animating into a cloud of wetware
self-connectedness. The standard
model is broke and the Cyborg
from the Assimulate, with a heart
of co-textual evaporate and the
big data noise of his eight or nine
minds at once, is out of the
amphitheatre and into the street.

This is the next big boy, so will
need a von Neumann schwabing
re-avatared into being, because
enlightened self interest and the
profit motive, aligned to Big Science
and the survival of the imperious,
are the best ways forward beyond
this realm, with its view cephalic,
on a course symphlitic, stalled
in the ABC of its own nostalgia.

There's a brave new world out there,
where the sun is but a quant mine
and the sky the very limpet, now
the Darwinian game's in play and our
Bot bot's reboot has set the path

already taken, to breach a door
through a wet brain e.fade and
recombinate the you, into the
technofictive mind we've all been
yearning for.

It's looking at us.

ROBERT SULLIVAN

Decolonising the Coastline

I'd been to Moeraki to see midges, kelp, waves
from Keri Hulme's *Moeraki Conversations*.
I sat in the rental car on the edge of the highway
at Waikouaiti. I did get out and walked
down the grassy bank over stones onto the sand.
There was a shag there like the ones on the skeletal pier
at Oamaru. I'd also seen a fur seal at Moeraki
which wasn't moving, just sixty metres
from the throng of tourists gathered around
the boulders that looked like biological
shape toys, too round to be eggs, hexagonal
lines spread on the surface waiting for the pieces.
I didn't photograph the seal so as not to draw attention
to her. The couple in the SUV next to me drove off.
That's when I started walking on the sand,
trying to remember Hulme's place names.

Pram Ride

I walked Turi around Sunnynook Park while a children's league team
played on the only open field. I saw a ten-year-old tackled to his knees

by five kids, and he limped off crying a few minutes later.
I kept watching; there was a really good girl who tackled players

fairly, and she was fast too, scoring a couple of tries. I watched
the other team struggle on as the girl's team scored several times.

It made wheeling the pram easier. Turi was fast asleep. We'd
had time to do a supermarket shop so I nibbled some seaweed

sheets out of sight of the players. Then I wheeled him back
as another huge tackle took down another youngster

who managed to stay in the game. I got caught up
in the excitement and yelled *Run!* But when a parent

smiled at me when another big tackle landed I walked away
and took Turi back home. I had no idea of the score.

Handsfree

A guy
from forty years in my past
was an energy saver.

He'd loop each thumb to its forefinger
so energy would recycle through his body.

Maybe that's why, on dates,
he never held my hand.

PAUL SCHIMMEL

The Right Place

Earth's the right place for love:
I don't know where it's likely to go better.
                                        —Robert Frost

New England, and they call it clapboard here.
A shingle drive through mid-summer woods
to where the grand Homer Noble House,
claps white and loud in meadow green.

A groundsman on a rattling ride-on mower,
no 'whispering' scythe to hear, dismounts:
yes, we can walk around, even visit Frost's
summer cabin; he proffers the key.

On the meadow rise the log cabin, retreat,
writing place, clay oven brown between wood
and open ground, does not call out, but draws
down the sun. I think of the groundsman

as Frost's everyman of earth and air,
of fire and ice; how the beginning was
and will be always, the logos, such words
the world holds, waiting to be found.

The cabin within is cool and sparse;
a simple bed, a shelf of books ... but here
the images fail. Would details hoarded
in a notebook, help now to make the poem?

Or is this more a work for faith: no school
save that of the self's experience,
of those moments, frozen, before pain; how
in his poems we feel, and hear again, each

detonation that has scarred the heart, the crack
of ice after winter has tried the earth;
how, out of chaos, this inarticulate infinite,
we, or the god in us, have created love.

Frost found his poems not so much
in the pain, but in the living of the pain;
in seasons of renewing his knowledge
there is, nowhere 'it's likely to go better'.

The Landfall Review

Landfall Review Online

www.landfallreview.com

Reviews posted since April 2019

(Reviewer's name in brackets)

Novel Origins?

by Shef Rogers

The Travels of Hildebrand Bowman, ed. Lance Bertelsen (Peterborough, Ontario, Canada: Broadview Press, 2016; distributed in Australasia by Footprint Books), 256pp, $38.25

Described on the back cover as 'the first New Zealand novel' and adorned with a photograph of a young Māori woman in a cloak, the anonymous fictional travels of Hildebrand Bowman have found a new audience thanks to the capable editing and extensive contextual materials that Lance Bertelsen brings to the text. Possessed of a title that would never mislead readers into believing the adventures (both the *Monthly* and *Critical Review* joked about the 'long bow' drawn by Bowman), the novel enjoyed a single edition in 1778 as part of the general fascination with Cook's voyages, then largely disappeared from the public imagination. With the publication of this edition, the book has become an ideal starting point for anyone interested in how South Sea discoveries were exploited by satirists of the day for contemporary social commentary. The novel has much to teach students about late eighteenth-century Britain, about European attitudes toward the Pacific, and about emerging ideas of race. I hope it will not be regarded as a source for understanding New Zealand, either as it was in Cook's day or as it is now, but it will certainly help New Zealanders understand the mindsets of the Europeans who first sailed to and wrote about Aotearoa.

Hildebrand Bowman purports to be a midshipman aboard the *Adventure* during Cook's second voyage, accidentally left behind when the rest of the landing party were massacred by Māori in Queen Charlotte Sound. Readers of the day would have already learned about the Grass Cove encounter from Cook's own account of the voyage, published in May 1777 by Strahan and Cadell, who brought out the novel the following year. Like Gulliver, the hero journeys through a series of societies, each of which satirises a different aspect of European culture by concentrating on different bodily senses. In the first society, Taupiniera, the people burrow amid squalor during the day, using their mole-like night vision to catch fish. Bowman then proceeds to Olfactaria, whose people reflect Māori practices in their use of facial tattoos and certain weapons, but who inform Bowman that those who killed his compatriots are a distinct cannibal tribe called the Carnovirrians. He next visits Auditante, whose residents enjoy exquisite hearing leading to great proficiency in music and poetry, and then arrives at Bonhommica, a nation echoing the culture of an idealised Tudor Britain, whose people abound in the 'sixth sense, but which they reckon the first ... the sense of conscience, or the moral sense' (p. 122). As Bertelsen points out in his valuable introduction, these societies are intended to represent the progression toward civilisation, moving from hunter-gatherer, through pastoral-nomadic, agricultural and commercial stages (p. 12), ultimately descending from commercial success into excessive luxury as Bowman leads a trading expedition to Luxo-Volupta (i.e. France), and from there finds a Dutch ship that enables him to return to England.

Such a summary makes The Travels sound like a novel of ideas, which it is, though it is a novel of late eighteenth-century ideas and fashions that have been, for the most part, superseded. Bertelsen has successfully rejuvenated the work through eight sets of appendices. Each appendix is prefaced by a headnote that contextualises the selections that follow, ranging in each case from two to seven items for a total of 40 historical passages that enable the modern reader to appreciate the book's implications and satire. By incorporating references to these appendices into both his lively introduction and the accompanying footnotes throughout the text, Bertelsen enables a reader to understand important debates of the day around theories on hierarchies of race, the relationship between trade and luxury, the importation of absurd French fashions, and historical knowledge about the Pacific and the search for the great southern continent. He also judiciously intersperses a total of 14 very clearly reproduced images throughout the text—images from Cook's voyage, from eighteenth-century cartoons, and from other novels that informed The Travels of

Hildebrand Bowman. The original edition of the novel included two pencil sketches that are reproduced here, but being able to see them alongside these other images (which the author no doubt knew) gives them a much greater depth and artistic potential than they enjoyed on their own.

Bertelsen also offers the most extensive discussion to date of the novel's authorship (pp. 35–39), building on previous work by Wellington bookseller Rowan Gibbs. The first possible candidate, John Elliott, sailed on Cook's second voyage as the Resolution's midshipman. The second candidate, Robert Home, was a modestly successful portrait painter who is most likely to have been the 'Mr. Home' who paid the printer for the 500 copies of the novel. The evidence for both is laid out clearly, but after the edition was published, Bertelsen had a chance to compare an inscribed copy of the novel auctioned at Sotheby's that has eliminated John Elliott on the basis of handwriting. Home has yet to be confirmed on the basis of handwriting, but remains the most likely author. Bertelsen might also have noted that were Elliott the author, it is hard to imagine him omitting this wonderful detail that he recorded in his surviving memoirs:

> Mr Banks came to Sheerness and when he saw the ship, and the Alterations that were made, He swore and stamp'd upon the Warfe, like a Mad Man; and he instantly ordr'd his servants, and all his things out of the Ship.

> (cited by Bertelsen, p. 56, n. 1)

Joseph Banks withdrew from Cook's second voyage when the Admiralty rejected as unseaworthy the modifications to the *Resolution* that Banks had demanded, but his tantrum on that occasion is not usually so vividly depicted.

Textually, the work follows the original edition very closely, 'except in cases where it seriously impeded understanding' (p. 45), a somewhat vague editorial policy but one that posed no obstacles to reading the text. The difficulties arise more from separating fact from fiction and appreciating the satiric implications. In the final paragraph of the book, Bowman requests that his countrymen 'will do me the honour' of naming the newly discovered lands either Bowmania or Hildebrandia (p. 181). Bertelsen explains that Bowman's Islands had been discussed in a 1774 work, *Sketches of the History of Man* by Lord Kames (1696–1782), which may have spurred the author's imagination, but the proposed name Bowmania also reinforces the novel's critique of colonialism as the enabler of deranged luxury. The author goes so far in his rejection of French fashions as to prefer the cross-dressing male actors in the theatrical productions of work by the most admired playwright of Bonhommica, Avonswan.

Even in 1778 the objections to colonialism were hardly novel, while women on the stage were no longer a topic of serious debate. And yet there are enough fascinating details and mentions of particular places and people that we somehow still wish for credibility. We therefore experience a certain thrill when we learn that the Sir Charles Saunders (c. 1715–1775), who repeatedly helped advance Bowman's career, is the same man after whom Cook had named Cape Saunders on the Otago Peninsula in 1770. So perhaps some readers will wish to continue to claim *The Travels of Hildebrand Bowman* as the first New Zealand novel, and we could do worse, now that Bertelsen and Broadview have made available such a rich and enticing edition.

A Dreamer of the Road
by Steve Braunias

Ghost South Road by Scott Hamilton, with photographs by Ian Powell and Paul Janman (Atuanui Press, 2018) 326pp, $59.99

Just after dawn one day in 2013 I set out to walk the Great South Road, heading, as the name commanded, south, for as far as I could make it before nightfall. Auckland's longest and most important road—the road to war, created by Governor Grey in 1862 to convey troops to the Waikato; as James Belich put it, 'It pointed like a giant sword at the heart of the Maori King movement'—begins at an intersection in expensive Newmarket, where great glassy emporiums filled with imported European cars mocked my journey on foot, and it ends somewhere or other in the Bombay Hills. One road: 33km in length. I interviewed passers-by and stopped for food, drink, birdwatching; I made it as far as Manurewa, 20.6km beneath my feet. I was quite proud of myself and wrote it up as a 3500-word story for *Metro* magazine. It was psychogeography, it was journalism, it was my own flat Everest. It was absolutely nothing compared to Dr Scott Hamilton: his book-length ode to Great South Road documents the year he spent walking the road, backwards and forwards, to and fro, dogged and immersive, in all covering—God almighty!—200km.

Those are some very hard yards indeed and there's a nice line in the book when he puts his feet up after a day's slog on Great South Road and notes that he has 'toothache in his heels'. He walked with his long-time collaborator, film-maker Paul Janman, whose photographs, together with images by cinematographer Ian Powell, illustrate the book in laconic black and white—a fenceline, a car wrecker's yard, a motorway bridge. There's also a 30-page photo section in colour of people and things, mostly things, in *Ghost South Road*.

Very cutely, he cites Heraclitus in his introductory chapter, when he quotes the old saw that nobody enters the same river twice; nobody, he ventures, travels the same Great South Road twice. My idea was to feel Auckland's pulse through the soles of my feet. I walked through well-appointed neighbourhoods, desperately poor neighbourhoods, zones of industry, zones of unrest, one suburb sprawling into the next, and listened to stories of Auckland lives. Hamilton's intent is at once dreamier and more purposeful. He wants to drag history—and injustice, conquest, colonial abuse—into the present. Mission splendidly accomplished.

The text is a series of essays written for specific occasions, and several are devoted to telling a history of the Waikato war. His book is a kind of rowdy, on-the-ground companion piece to Vincent O'Malley's monumental and scholarly work, *The Great War for New Zealand: Waikato 1800–2000*. Hamilton's approach is scholarly too. He's good at sourcing small, personal details from the past and interpreting their meaning. Something else, though, is at work in *Ghost South Road*. The essays read like a prose-poem. His book is an artistic enterprise.

Interesting guy. Hamilton operates as a public intellectual without much of a public. He's cult, freelance, an author of obscure works—I loved his 2017 book, a slim, elegant, powerful essay published by Bridget Williams Books, *The Stolen Island*, an investigation into the people-snatching raid on the Tongan island of `Ata in 1863. Hamilton qualifies as an old Pacific hand. He brings an angry intelligence to his subject. A few years ago he tore comedian and broadcaster Te Radar a new one in his review of the 2012 light-ent series *Radar Across the Pacific*, writing in his exhilarating blog Reading the Maps that the travel show was full of 'racist cliches' and 'hoary ethnic stereotypes'. The show's director, Peter Bell, posted a rather condescending defence on the blog, and Hamilton promptly tore him a new one too.

Hamilton is on intimate terms with anger. One of the most closely observed set-pieces in the book describes a furious cup of tea with the great South Island songwriter Bill Direen. A wrong word sends Direen into a cold, seething rage. I know Bill and regard him with the utmost respect bordering on fear. Hamilton clearly reveres him—many people do; he was the subject of the reverential and really quite unquestioning 2017 documentary

A Memory of Others—and it's an interesting decision to include that storm in a teacup. It doesn't add anything to our understanding of the Great South Road. It's got nothing to do with the Great South Road. Well, what of it? It gets to Direen, illuminates something about the artiste. In fact there's a sense that the book is more about art than the Great South Road.

'I have been guided, throughout my adventures, by artists,' Hamilton forewarns in the Introduction. Yes, yes, sorry for the emotive word, but I took it as a warning: art yap lies ahead. It duly arrived. Some of it's good yap. Hamilton is particularly insightful on the nineteenth-century Great South Road photographer William Temple, and his portrait of Direen, set against the Waikato, is fascinating. Then there's this yap about an exhibition of Māori art in a gallery in Papakura: 'The turnout for … the opening was disappointing, and I wondered if it had something to do with local history.' He then sails off to contemplate the Waikato war, and draws a bow that colonial rule fostered a long-lasting neglect of Māori. But oh c'mon. Who wants to go to an art gallery in Papakura? All art is just some things in a room and there are so many diversions or better things to do than attend an opening in a pastoral suburb—sport, TV, dinner, drugs, bed.

He takes it all so seriously. Art, literature, deep thoughts are everywhere. 'I thought of Borges's story,' he claims, while watching Direen and his band rock out at a gig. 'I thought of Borges's story,' he claims, again, at Janman's idea of creating a website-map of every stationary object along Great South Road.

The sight of a concrete mixer makes him think of a military cannon left behind by a retreating army: 'I imagined the trucks, diggers and graders [in Pokeno] as tanks, patrolling a captured town.' Things, things, things. Where are the people?

Answer: in art galleries. Hamilton writes about a video installation at a gallery in Pukekohe. Salome Tanuvasa's film *Expensive Movements* shows a hotel cleaner stripping beds. 'It made me think about …' etc etc—at least it wasn't another Borges story. He could just as easily have met and spoken to an actual living hotel cleaner on his walk. Hamilton writes in his Introduction that he interviewed 'arborists, publicans'. I'd have loved to heard from them but one of the few working people he talks to is his neighbour.

Further regarding Tanuvasa's film, he climbs up high on a moral horse and compares it, derisively, to a photograph by ex-*Herald* snapper Brett Phibbs of a woman picking onions in a field near the Great South Road in Ramarama. The photo dehumanises her, Hamilton seethes. Well, this is a bit rich. I know Phibbsy. He worked at the *Herald* for approximately 200 years, bloody legend, and one thing about him was his empathy and compassion for people. Hamilton, picking his delicate way

around art galleries hither and yon, sipping on white wine and contemplating the cube of cheese harpooned to an olive, is only able to summon his outrage because Phibbsy had bothered to go into the fields to take the photo in the first place.

I wish Hamilton had gone into pubs and got into fights, argued, defended, attacked or just plain engaged with the people of Great South Road. For someone who walked its length and then some, he's a curiously distant figure in his own book, an academic ('Professor Hamilton', as Direen teases him) with his head in the clouds. A dreamer of the road: but that's the considerable virtue of the book too.

Hamilton is a singular kind of rooster. He's captivated by art practice, by artefacts, their true or distorted mirrors of society and culture. It's exhilarating to follow the ways his mind is let loose on Great South Road, the connections he makes with scrub and swamp, with ancient pā and the fallen dead. His book is a resurrection of sorts, placing the Waikato war in a modern context: 'One Friday night not long ago I stepped out of a shop in Otahuhu. Rain was falling; traffic had jammed up, time had unspooled. The campervan in front of me was a supply wagon stuck in Victorian mud. Queuing cars shuddered like horses before a charge. The service station across the road burned orange, like a church or redoubt under attack.'

I don't believe a word of it, frankly. I don't think he did have those amazing visions. They seem contrived, made up—do queued cars really shudder like horses? It reads like a literary conceit; I suspect he was no more likely to have been possessed of that thought than he claims to have been reminded of a Borges story during Direen's gig at a small, stinking hot cellar on K Road. (I was there. I went with broadcaster Graeme Hill, who whirled like a dervish and accidentally punched Hamilton in the face.)

But an over-active or worked-at imagination is better than no imagination at all. *Ghost South Road* is a one-off; a strange, rare achievement; a road trip into the past guided by Hamilton's brilliant and erratic mind. It goes places that most New Zealand literature can't reach. It's possibly even a minor classic. It's definitely one for the ages.

The Safe Coat of Becoming

by Elizabeth Smither

James K. Baxter: Letters of a poet, vols 1 & 2, ed. John Weir (Victoria University Press, 2019), 800 + 848pp, $100

My one sighting: James Keir Baxter, James K. Baxter, Baxter, Hemi, gliding along Manners Street some time in the sixties. Bare feet, toenails untrimmed and black, ancient parka, eyes hooded but hypnotic. (Look at me if you dare; there's danger here.)

JKB salutations: Dear Mother; Dear Mother and Daddy; Dear Noel (Ginn); Dear Sir, 'I herewith append my statement in support of my appeal on conscientious grounds'; Dear Allen (Curnow), 'Excuse the Christian name'; Dear Phyl (Ferrabee); Darling Baby Snookums (Jacquie Baxter).

JKB signings: All best wishes, James; Love and best wishes, Jum; Fond regards, JKB; I dreamt of you last night, darling. Jim; Yours affectionately, James. Most commonly, Love Jim. Often simply: Jum.

A photograph: Baxter with his coat on backwards in Cathedral Square at the New Zealand Writers' Conference in 1951. Already the cynosure of all eyes. The prodigal tree among all the academic redwoods with their legs in Oxford bags like trunks.

Noel Ginn, Baxter's earliest correspondent outside family, makes a suggestion, to which Baxter responds, 'What you say about me needing friends, not admirers, hits one nail on the head. But friends are more uncomfortable than admirers ...' (To Noel Ginn, Whitanui. 3 June 1944). While Curnow's opinion, with provocation, might settle to 'a thoroughly vulgar little libido', Charles Brasch, in the early years would 'go about repeating to myself, with joy and wonder that this should have sprung out of New Zealand'.

Always Baxter had a metaphor to hand. 'The perfect metaphor for poetry is egg-laying. The poem has the oneness, the smooth outer surface of the egg, the inside meat made of the poet's mind. And if kept and warmed in the minds of others it may flower into a living chicken' (To Noel Ginn. 25 February 1944). In the quarrel with Curnow a pig came in handy. 'The pig must have a right to squeal if its throat is being cut—the pig in this case is N.Z. poetry.'

As Baxter's rather masterly editorial dealings at School Publications illustrate, he had the requisite flattering skills. He could smooth feathers when writers of school bulletins produced work that needed scissoring or re-conceiving for a juvenile audience; his letters adopt a conspiratorial tone, rather like modern creative writing teaching: praise, criticise, praise. And there can be a self-seeking directness and boldness in presuming publication that has long disappeared. Start with 'Just a note to say how much I liked the last *Landfall*' (to Brasch) or 'Dear Sarge, I salute you!' (to

Frank Sargeson). Poems would be dispatched, copies of his Macmillan Brown lectures, with a suitably modest disclaimer: 'I always feel on the defensive because of the lack of system in my thinking ...' Charles Brasch, an acute reader of the literary tea leaves, would periodically send a cheque.

Always this mix of strategy and chaos, for JKB was a writer who had a deliberate hand in his fate. Or he took care to assemble a 'bag of little foxes [to] spoil the vine'. Alcoholism and AA, anarchy and 'my happy little Civil Servant cell', marriage, abstinence and rape all rolled into an unholy ball. He recognised his own stubbornness, his garrulity. The things he tried—university degree, postman, 'School Pubs', smutty (but enjoyable) ballads, Catholicism—were done in batches. In fact they might have been on playback:

Can I say without a cough
Expecting you not to laugh—
Love me till I die,
Love me for what I am?
Terribly dangerous talk
Even if said in fun.

'Song for a Christmas Cracker'

The Auckland–Wellington schism, still in relatively good heart, and the drawn-out quarrel over Curnow's selection for *The Penguin Book of New Zealand Verse* produced a letter of unusual bluntness: 'I do wish, though, to register the strongest possible protest against your increasingly subjective judgement of the value of the work of other New Zealand poets.' To miss out on inclusion in such a major anthology must have seemed like missing the bus and not knowing when the next would be along. Everything had to be created: bus, driver, foreign sponsor, authoritative introduction. Not a country bus travelling over rough roads, but one that would be noticed in London or wherever poetry was read. The Wellington poets seem more buccaneering; Baxter's letter withdrawing his work has a hand on the dagger. Perhaps he thought Miss Eunice Frost at Penguin Books could be browbeaten. In the event she just withdrew until the fires died down.

Catholicism with its rich labyrinths and hierarchical structures (Virgin Mary accepted) had a natural appeal for Baxter. 'You know I am too inclined to run to Mass as a rabbit runs to its burrow,' he writes to Phyl Ferrabee. Its appeal parallels the developments in his writing, the knotted and abstract suddenly and miraculously bursting through into a real New Zealand flora and fauna, poems about clear water and hills, the solitude of a new land, having a heart of anger that feels pure and transforming. Sometimes the sharp details feel like iron.

But there was a price to pay in his closest relationship, his marriage to Jacquie Sturm. 'By God, the marriage set-up is hard going at any time!' he writes to Phyl. 'The hooks and eyes of relationships just slide.' Or he describes it as 'A shared endurance test, not a garden of Greek statues'. But there are times of contentment too: 'Things are pretty good with us,' he writes to Richard Thompson. There are loving, acutely detailed descriptions of their children, Hilary and John. The months they spent in India were healing, albeit celibate ones. So often it is Millicent Baxter's analysis that is nearest the truth. Baxter writes, 'I remember your saying to me once, not long before Jacquie and I separated, something to the effect that the basic problem of our marriage was probably that I did not love Jacquie completely and whole-heartedly.'

> I learnt from reading Freud and Jung
>   And several other pundits
> That repressions not transgressions
>   Had clogged my human conduits.

'Ballad of the Holy Ghost'

At times I had an image of letters burned or charred at the edges. Too many letters from School Publications, too few from other periods or situations. In early letters to Noel Ginn there is a mutual vaunting of talent—'truly great poetry' … 'approaches genius'—but criticism from Noel is swiftly deflected; you can sense the text turning away. Baxter was not a poet who listened much.

Was it Gerard Manley Hopkins scurrying along Willis Street? Or Guy Fawkes on his way to a conspirators' meeting at the George? *Dear Lou. My dear old perverted friend.* After the jugs went around, lines for a ballad might be dashed down on a coaster. Then home to Jacquie and the children, a tender observation in a letter to Phyl. But the road to Jerusalem was as enduring as the red thread that steered Theseus out of the

Minotaur's labyrinth. At the end of the thread were the Jerusalem sonnets. By a strange transubstantiation the poems become clearer, more brilliant and at ease as the sense of humbug in the letters grows.

> Yesterday I planted garlic,
> Today, sunflowers—'the non-essentials first'
>
> Is a good motto—but these I planted in honour of
> The Archangel Michael and my earthly friend
>
> Illingworth, Michael also, who gave me the seeds—
> And they will turn their pure wild golden discs
>
> Outside my window, following Te Ra
> Who carries fire for us in his terrible wings
>
> (Heresy, man!)—and if He wanted only
> For me to live and die in this old cottage
>
> It would be enough, for the angels who keep
> The very stars in place resemble most
>
> These green brides of the sun, hopelessly in love
> With their Master and Maker, drunkards of the sky.
>
> – Hemi

The flow and beauty of this writing has hardly been surpassed in New Zealand or anywhere else. It captures the real heart of poetry which is like a disappearance into the subject that is discovered and illuminated as line follows line. 'The green brides of the sun', which will turn golden, as they rotate.

James K. Baxter: Letters of a poet is so beautifully produced it puts the *School Journal's* prescription to shame. In its two-volume box set, front, back and sides graced by Nigel Brown's art, it reminds me of a relic. Is it worth $100? Undoubtedly. John Weir's introduction is a considered masterpiece. The layout, notes and references are elegant and easy to use. Are they the best letters ever written? Certainly not. Baxter's considering rape as marital therapy is enough to disqualify them. It is a failure of imagination so gross it spills onto other pages. There are times when introversion and self-absorption are so extreme the hard-to-define kind of charm that letters require to be memorable is impossible. Better perhaps to regard it as a journey of coats, the coat worn backwards, the old anorak and finally, in 'Poem for Colin 6', 'the safe coat of becoming'.

Three Praise Singers

by Michael Steven

Keeping a Grip by Kevin Ireland (Steele Roberts, 2019), $20; **The Moon in a Bowl of Water** by Michael Harlow (Otago University Press, 2019), 80pp, $27.50; **One Hundred Poems and a Year** by Bob Orr (Steele Roberts, 2018), $29.99

In the pantheon of senior New Zealand writers Kevin Ireland is one of our last great literary pugilists. *Keeping a Grip*, his 25th collection, arrives in his 85th year. He goes on duking it. Of his generation, only C.K. Stead, another type of literary brawler, matches him in poetic output. Here are 61 poems spread across three sections: 'Morning Reports; Midday Bulletins; News at Midnight'. Ireland's own drawing on the cover—a right-handed fist clutching a pencil—serves as a reasonably accurate summation of his current poetic.

The act of the poem has indeed become a routine of 'keeping a grip' on the world (and these poems are full of worldliness), and a way of staying tethered to the things that fill a life. There is a casual dailiness to this sort of writing—as if each poem written were shoring up some small victory over the long silence of a life's inevitable terminus. It is no surprise, then, to find the majority of the poems in this book are light lyrics and occasional, anecdotal verse. Ireland has a gift for the direct, declarative statement. No fireworks, no

histrionics. He also shares a simpatico with the grounded, earnest lyricism found in, say, Michael Longley or Paul Durcan. Here is the first stanza of a short poem entitled 'Dinner Last Night':

Dinner last night, simple
but superb. As man and wife
we watched it cook and waved
a corkscrew.

Many of the poems in *Keeping a Grip* celebrate eating and drinking, and the twin aegises of solidarity and intimacy they facilitate. A confession: I've been a sucker for food poems ever since I read of Gary Snyder braising a stew in Mexico's Pinacate desert—especially when the poem functions as a recipe. First published in The Spinoff's Friday Poem anthology, Ireland's 'Lamb Stew with Bonus' is an absolute cracker of an instructional for an evening of Epicurean togetherness. In my estimation it ranks with Ian Wedde's 'Ode 1.3 to Bill Culbert and Ralph Hotere: Art Noir' and Hone Tuwhare's 'Friend', as one of our best examples of literary food writing.

Ireland is, above all, a slinger of sly stories: an Aesop of the winebar anecdote. And the best of the poems collected here attest to a talent for well-wrought fabulations—for the telling of yarns that couch or scaffold some gentle moral or philosophical truth. He is careful, though, to evade a common danger, one that befalls even the most cunning of raconteurs: telling the same story twice, with differing incidentals. If I have one criticism of this collection, it is that the lesser poems are perhaps weakened when the poetry itself has been obfuscated by the exercise of its writing. But if one has spent the majority of a life writing poems, and is still actively doing so in the middle of one's eighth decade, they just might be worth listening to—especially when the wisdom espoused is this hard tempered:

Advising the Young

I have never been floored by the thought that because the readership for poetry is small (except during wars or collective moments of pain or exultant notoriety) this was an adequate excuse for not getting on with the job of scratching out a response to what often seems to be only an irritant—a drumming in the mind.

My heart goes out to the young victims of the need to fire off cryptic messages to an unkind world. There's little money and less fame and the personal price is sometimes hardly worth it. I have to tell them that my best advice is not to have a bar of it. I keep to myself the good news of the pleasure. That's for them to find.

*

If the figure of Perseus were attributed a single literary form it would, undoubtedly, be the prose poem. From its origins in Lu Chi's Wen Fu, the prose poem has slithered through time, back and forth across continents and literary genres. Poet Stephen Oliver brings to my attention Gerard Manley Hopkins' prose descriptions of the dramatic effects Krakatoa's explosion had on British skies. There is Walt Whitman's appropriation of the form in Specimen Days, his account of the American Civil War. Rabindranath Tagore, the great Indian pre-modernist, composed his masterwork Gitanjali in short prose units. Even the German Romantics Hölderlin and Heine tried their hand at the form—largely as an act of rebellion against the strictures and rules of versification. And then, of course, there are the French Symbolist masters: Baudelaire, Mallarmé, Rimbaud, through to the phenomenologist Francis Ponge. Let us not forget, either, the lineage of Latin American practitioners—a line running from Jorge Luis Borges, by way of Julio Cortázar and Clarice Lispector, through to the experimental novels of Roberto Bolaño and César Aira. Theorists and critics such as Walter Benjamin (One-way Street) and Jean Baudrillard (Cool Memories 1980–1985) have also had a go. Essayists, too, such as John Berger, Annie Dillard, Eliot Weinberger, and younger prose stylists like Teju Cole and Maggie Nelson have all utilised the form to some extent in their writings.

This is not a history of the prose poem—I am merely offering a glimpse of the form's proliferation and multiplicity. Because the prose poem is again having a moment—this time in the guise of 'flash fiction'. I have before me two collections of poetry by Michael Harlow: Nothing but Switzerland and Lemonade (published in 1980 by Alan Loney's Hawk Press), and his twelfth and latest, The Moon in a Bowl of Water. Both are volumes of prose poems. Nearly 40 years of writing extend between these two books. Harlow, then, is likely New Zealand's most consistent and accomplished practitioner of the form. Harlow the writer is also something of a Perseus.

In these poems we find flashes of actual and imagined biography. Harlow is a bricoleur: gathering shards of mythological narrative—narratives, at once familiar and unknowably alien to us. He cobbles together filigrees of unthought thoughts, and fragmented meditations on the creative act. Mystery abounds in The Moon; so does psychoanalytical insight. It also presents a deep awareness of the shadowy enterprise of the poetic act:

> Beneath the poem you have just written, there
>   is always the poem
> you might have written. Entering the house of
>   poetry by the front
> door, wind chimes a musical call, you leave
>   by the back door.
> And you discover who you are again, but
>   someone
> else as well. You discover that you are now
>   inside the poem you
> might have written—bringing the far, more
>   near.

The above poem ('Short Talk on the "Far More Near"') is the last in the collection, and is an exemplification of Harlow's gifts. He is playful, while also philosophical. The tumblings and turnings of his mind-in-thought are redolent of Wallace Stevens or John Ashbery, without the latter's annoying torpor.

Harlow's poetry abounds with arcane allusion and esoteric symbolism. He is a careful host, though, and the collection is appended with useful notes to elucidate his texts.

*

From the outset, I will declare this: Bob Orr's ninth collection One Hundred Poems and a Year is nothing short of a triumph. Like Homer, Melville, Crane, Olson and Curnow, Orr is a poet for whom the ocean is a psychic nexus. An imago mundi of sorts. A place where at any given instant of time the world's history entire converges. He spent 40 years as a mariner: piloting container and cruise ships through the jewelled archipelagos of the Hauraki Gulf and Waitemata Harbour. It makes sense that Orr's poetic intelligence is founded on the rhythms, accents, moods and weathers of the ocean, and that these forces have shaped his writing. But Orr's poetic education started much earlier. This, from 'Heliotropes':

> A farmer's son
> exchanging one dusty road for
>
> another
> once bought an edition
> of Penguin Modern European Poets:
> Four Greek Poets
> Cavafy
> Elytis
> Gatsos
> and
> Seferis
> from the mezzanine floor
> of Paul's Book Arcade
> Hamilton.

Orr is a son of the Waikato. In 2017 he spent the year as Writer in Residence at the University of Waikato where, according to the blurb, most of his new collection was written. Anyone familiar with his previous books will know him as a poet who never strays far from the hearth of the human heart. He is, like the two previous poets, a praise singer. It is rare (except maybe in the poems of Cavafy, Reznikoff or Tranströmer) to encounter such a pure, unaffected lyricism—and one of such luminous concision. Whether he is writing of friends, landscapes, potatoes or Jonah Lomu, his eye is ever clear, and always compassionate.

Earlier, I declared this book a triumph. Here's why: It is, among many other things, a book about grief. It is a book about how we navigate ourselves through grief, and beyond into that difficult territory of intractable associations the departed leave us with. 'The River' (p. 44) is the masterpiece of the collection. While the poet sits with his wife in her dying moments, he is attuned to the physiology of her body shutting down. Here is the birth of a grief. Uncannily, he marries the progression of the psyche leaving the body with a meditation on the Waikato River, moving in its course outside the hospital window, comparable to Lucretius in its irrefutable and cosmic truth. It is impossible here to do the poem justice by quoting snippets. In an age of discordant, distractive noise and hyperbole, Orr's voice is the clear voice of love. And we are better off for hearing it.

Day of Reckoning
by Mark Broatch

Pearly Gates by Owen Marshall (Vintage, 2019), 288pp, $38

Pat Gates, known even to his late mother as Pearly, runs a thriving real estate business in a provincial town in the South Island. He would be the first to tell you he's a former Otago rugby player who might have gone all the way apart from a few injuries at the wrong time. More importantly, he's the mayor, considering going for a third term. 'You'll bolt in again,' someone says early on. But will he? Most people seem to like him, though he knows you can't but help make a few enemies in a job like his.

There are rural parades and loving depictions of farm life. People are called 'jokers' and 'roosters'. We're in Owen Marshall country. The mode is realist, masculine, mostly Pākehā, heavy on character and place, lighter on plot—Pearly briefly travels to Auckland and Christchurch but otherwise remains in the quiet, steady streets of his town—and interested in moral and emotional truths.

Best known for his rightly praised short stories, Marshall has written a handful of novels, the arguably 'off-canon' *Harlequin Rex* winning the top fiction prize in its year.

At the novel's centre are Pearly and his wife Helen, both in their early sixties, who have long since settled into a familiar pattern. Their children have left home, the slightly wayward, larky son in Auckland doing something with boat cruises, the beloved gynaecologist daughter and grandkids far away in England. Pearly and Helen rely on each other, happily talk past each other. She is his rock, his behind-every-good-man, his answering machine, his plus-one. There is little, though, in the way of romance or sex. It's not that they don't love each other, you feel, just that their affection is expressed in less showy ways.

Pearly admits he's a bit hazy on some of Helen's hopes and worries, putting that down to his perpetual busyness. 'Proximity in itself is no guarantee of understanding,' the novel notes. She has a close friend who is encouraging her to go back to nursing—and who it seems effectively does some of the emotional work of the marriage. After realising that his wife probably does want to resume her career, Pearly resolves to be more supportive and caring, and is immediately pleased with himself for this resolution.

He prides himself on his reliability, his going the extra mile, his ability to say the right thing on every occasion. He's a man who understands how the worlds of politics and business work, adroit at playing those roles, while staying in touch with the very real concerns of the common bloke. For instance, he knows as mayor and realtor that suburban infill is sensible, but that this often makes once-fine homes awkwardly confined, 'like a zoo giraffe enclosed with an orphaned hippopotamus'.

The writing in *Pearly Gates*—the story told largely through the words and eyes of our protagonist—is not usually keen to draw attention to itself. People are introduced with a few revealing details and traits. Some have splendid names: Snoz Gazler, Chimp Thwaites, Gwendolyn Posswillow. A wry humour sits just below the surface. Occasionally you'll get a line that reminds you that Marshall is also a poet. 'The sun had gone down on its knees and flamed through the line of macrocarpas at the end of the grounds.' Or: 'He had glimpsed the dark, scaly tail of something implacable and self-serving in his nature and feared its entirety.' The dialogue is spare, honing character, pushing things along.

> 'One woman there, Chrissie, she invited me for dinner because I jump-started her Nissan. She talked a lot about living on her own and things going wrong. A nice person, but I'm not used to listening for so long to personal stuff. What can you say about other people's troubles?'
> 'Take her out to a movie or something.'
> 'She's got this habit of showing her teeth when she's unhappy.'
> 'Make her feel better, then,' said Pearly. 'Do her garden for her, or fix the taps.'
> 'She can cook all right, and she's not fat at all.'
> 'There you are then,' said Pearly.

Even though Pearly seems pleased with his lot, career and marriage, that's not to say he has no unseemly desires; the odd comment or action that might have at one time been dismissed as silly-old-fool behaviour could now be regarded as something more grave.

Would he truly transgress? He's known the blinding power of infatuation, the humiliating pain of rejection. He has seen first hand that love may 'provide sublime happiness or occasion a total collapse of an ordered life'.

In fact he does step over a moral boundary, though it's not in pursuit of the flesh. He makes a questionable self-interested call, seemingly out of character. Or perhaps it's just a seldom seen, less examined part of his personality. As a result, a slightly foreboding mood settles over the second half of the book. Something's on its way, comeuppance perhaps. Someone begins stalking him on the phone. Does this have anything to do with his deed? A couple of arson attacks occur. Is everything connected? Or is it merely his rising guilt?

Pearly still reminisces about his glory days. Partly this is about his ego, which, despite his best efforts, remains fulsome. But also, this is his 'brand'. He wouldn't have become mayor without his minor fame, his farming background, his assiduously assembled standing in the community. There is no mention of what will happen when he finally does hand back the mayoral chains—or anything beyond that. Even if Marshall has the ability to let that thought slip quietly through the vents. Pearly's nickname naturally brings to mind one's day of reckoning, when St Peter checks off our earthly deeds in his big book, potentially stopping us getting through those giant pearly gates. Pearls of wisdom comes to

mind, too: Pearly readily dispenses these—even to himself, dishing out regular pep talks after some lapse: 'Jesus, Pearly.'

Some chapters end with a page or two of italicised text that offer further insight into Pearly's deepest thoughts, dreams, an alternative existence. It's not quite Craig Marriner-level-intrusive, but it isn't entirely clear to me why it's set off in this way. Perhaps it's so the author can sneak in more lines like this: 'Their cars would be drawn under the drapery of the trees to escape the sun, and in the open riverbed the greywacke stones would shimmer and the clumps of broom and lupin and gorse tough it out with no relief.'

If there's a unifying incident to the novel, it's the local school's upcoming 125th celebrations. An esteemed guest is flying in—someone whose appearance will have an unsettling, though salutary, effect on Pearly. As will an accident. This late flurry of events only serves to remind us how little has gone on before. But the author is of course more interested in what we can learn from the life of the individual, the usually unnoticed crests and troughs of the everyday.

As we approach the final chapters, more Marshall perennials arise. Will Pearly do the right thing? How much of what's gone on is his fault, and how much is random chance? Will he, can he, change? Pearly's not really a bad bloke, is he?

Challenging Patriarchal Amnesia

by Jocelyn Harris

The Political Years by Marilyn Waring (Bridget Williams Books, 2019), 376pp, $39.99

In the interests of full disclosure, I declare that I like and admire Marilyn Waring. Now, after reading *The Political Years* at one gulp, I'm quite simply awestruck by her principles, courage, intelligence, stamina, and saving sense of the ridiculous.

How on earth did she cope with Robert Muldoon? One day, wanting to show my children democracy in action, I took them to Parliament, where the prime minister was jeering and sneering away like a teenager just asking to be sent to his room. I happened to have a large drumhead cabbage in my bag, and my fingers itched to pot him with it. A single, brief exposure and I was ready to snap, but Waring endured him year after wearisome year.

On the black and white cover of *The Political Years* a young woman stands solitary in a phalanx of men, many of them old. A thin red line points to the anomaly. Waring's friends, constituents, correspondents and some of her parliamentary colleagues would be generous in support, but relentless and often vicious pressure came from other MPs, anonymous trolls and the media. The loathsome *New Zealand Truth* even outed her as a lesbian at a time when New Zealand was deeply homophobic. 'Part of me was broken,' she writes, but 'something reckless was also unleashed in me, and I would use that energy for the issues ahead' (p. 67).

Use that energy she certainly did. In the belief that feminism was broader and more encompassing than party politics, Waring crossed the floor and discussed matters of conscience with Opposition politicians. In her usual prophetic way she urged long-term planning to protect the environment from natural climatic changes and industry, to look at our whole internal transport system, and to recognise that the Pacific would become 'the crux of our foreign policy' (p. 69). And she spoke up passionately for women, arguing in 1976, for instance, that 'when a person is murdered, the murderer is put on trial but when a woman is raped, it is the woman who is put on trial' (p. 61).

Waring always did her homework, recording events and conversations in clippings, letters, notes and diaries that she wasn't supposed to keep. That way she could compare 'what was said and agreed in caucus, and what Muldoon told the media and the public' (p. 78). She also spoke knowledgeably on a dizzying array of topics including 245T, Agent Orange, alternative energy, Bastion Point, divorce, domestic violence, education, employment, homosexuality and the Colin Moyle affair, housing, human rights, land rights, nuclear power, overstayers, parental leave, parliamentary boundaries, parliamentary reform, privatisation, rural depopulation, sales tax, shop trading hours, urban planning, unionism, water, and youth rates. But she was largely ignored. 'Bigoted and anachronistic laws' were upheld and 'difficult decisions postponed for another day', leaving her 'cynically resigned to hopelessness' (p. 70).

On women's health, for instance, the distance between MPs' understanding and women's evidence-based research was 'galactic', writes Waring (p. 82), especially about abortion. The government was plotting to limit access even further, but she argued that since justice was 'considerably slower than procreation', women would find it faster and cheaper to seek out illegal abortionists. Parliament voted late at night, Muldoon could not remember what he had voted for or when, and all of George Gair's compromise amendments were lost.

Looking back, though no longer in anger, Waring writes that her political autobiography challenges 'the dominant "history" of the period; it breaks the silence and challenges patriarchal amnesia' (p. 9). In short, it bears witness. She makes of her 'visceral memories' (p. 8) a page-turning and sometimes hilarious narrative, even though her lists of activities would make most people clutch their heads and scream. A list chosen at random reads: 'visiting pine-forest nurseries, plastics factories, electric-fence manufacturers, retirement villages, rest homes, and the Church of the Latter Day Saints school and village in Tuhikaramea. I went to Geoff Chitty's bull sale in the Waikaretu Valley' (p. 29). She kept on top of it all, primed and ready to contribute.

In 1974 Waring had joined National on impulse after Norman Kirk refused to support any legislation that treated homosexuality as 'normal behaviour'. Though introduced at the Raglan selection meeting as the 'wonderful candidate Marilyn Monroe' (p. 30), she won the seat handsomely. The New Zealand Woman's Weekly, unable to abandon its stereotypical thinking, described her as a 'girl, brown-eyed, honey-blonde', with 'a mischievous giggle'. Even when talking 'earnestly on a subject close to her heart, Marilyn's voice is scarcely raised. She is a lot gentler, prettier than newspaper articles and photographs have indicated' (p. 54). Waring was both Muldoon's youth card and his token woman. 'I wanted a woman,' said he, 'and I will help all I can' (p. 19). It didn't last.

Photographs illustrate some of Waring's most urgent concerns—carrying a box of petitions asking for reform of the abortion laws up the steps of Parliament; moving a plaque commemorating 75 years of women's suffrage from a back corridor to a more prominent location; joining protesters at the Hamilton game of the 1981 Springbok tour; and leaving her office on 13 June 1984 for the debating chamber, where she would cross the floor on Richard Prebble's Nuclear Free New Zealand Bill.

Waring tells a riveting inside story about the Bill. Although it had already gained a majority, Muldoon stopped it from going to Executive Council to be signed by the governor-general. For Waring, as for Opposition MPs Helen Clark, Wallace Rowling and Jonathan Hunt, that was an appalling threat to democracy, but the Speaker shut her out of the debate. With the National Party holding a majority of one, resignation was not an option. Instead, she withdrew from caucus and all her committees.

'Just what do you think you are up to now, you perverted little liar?' demanded Muldoon, swilling down glass after glass of brandy and ginger. 'If you say that again outside the room I will sue the shit out of you,' returned Waring, munching on an apple. Muldoon accused her of lying, of being 'just after headlines to please her lefty feminist friends' (pp. 341–42), then announced a snap election in his infamous drunken press conference. Waring refused to accept the blame, thinking to herself, 'You will have to fight on your lousy leadership, poor economic management, and abusive personality' (p. 343). Labour won, and the Nuclear Free New Zealand Bill passed into law.

The grind eventually drove Waring to the limit. Being part of the party under Muldoon was 'extremely dark' (p. 233), she writes, especially in the 'very crazy period' of the 1981 rugby tour when 'hypocrisies, lies and double standards were all in evidence as we engaged the nightmare' (p. 245). She swam and she ran and she knitted furiously, but the stress brought on weeping and vomiting. Ashamed and despairing about her enforced complicity with the government's abuse of foreign leaders, its public release of SIS information about protesters and its 'breathtaking lack of integrity and principle in the name of holding a few rural seats' (p. 251), she held her public and private lives together until the day the vacuum cleaner broke down, then she slumped to the floor, back to the wall, unable to move. Luckily, her GP happened to come by and sent her to a private hospital for a rest. Waring's dreams of raising goats on a paradisal farm became more and more vivid, and she handed in her resignation.

Outside New Zealand Waring's reputation grew exponentially, and in 1980 she received a standing ovation in Copenhagen for speaking feminism in New Zealand's name at a UN Conference on Women. Long before the word 'intersectionality' was invented, she explained how women were oppressed in multiple, overlapping ways. On a fellowship to Harvard in 1981 she relished conversations with like-minded people, and in 1984 she published her hugely influential economic treatise *Counting for Nothing*. Here she explained that to measure success by the Gross National Product is to overlook the trillion-dollar contribution of unpaid workers such as mothers, rural women, caregivers and volunteers. More than three decades later our current government is busily replacing the GDP with more inclusive indicators.

As Waring once said, 'It was unfortunate that I was elected to Parliament with a mind, and I'm going to use it, but it doesn't make people happy' (p. 325). Muldoon tried to break her spirit and wear her down, but as a constitutional commentator explained, the role of caucus is 'to challenge Prime Ministers to think again. There is no other body to provide such a check on the political executive.' Marilyn Waring, the 'conscientious and competent' back-bencher, 'understood this and acted on it', he said (p. 323). That was the job she was elected to do, and she did it. Some youth card, some token woman.

Find your sensation and put a line around it

by David Eggleton

Frances Hodgkins: European journeys,
eds Catherine Hammond and Mary Kisler
(Auckland University Press, 2019), 268pp, $75

In the middle of the twentieth century, New Zealand-born artist Frances Hodgkins (1879–1947) was located right at the heart of the British art avant-garde, and arguably the most significant and the most fêted woman painter in Britain at the time. In 1939 she was selected by Sir Kenneth Clark, director of the National Gallery in London, to show her work in the British Pavilion at the New York World's Fair, and later that year the British Council invited her to exhibit her work in the British Pavilion at the 1940 Venice Biennale, eventually cancelled because of World War II.

In 1945 she was included in a group exhibition at Lefevre Galleries, London, with Francis Bacon, Henry Moore, Matthew Smith and Graham Sutherland. Critics in art magazines and newspapers declared her one of the most remarkable woman painters of the time. Eric Newton wrote: 'Hers is a twilight colour. It is queer and surprising. Moreover, it continues to be surprising. Looking at her best gouaches, the eye, long after first impact, goes on receiving little subsidiary shocks of delight.' A younger artist, Cedric Morris, spoke of her as 'completely unconventional ... witty in a strange oblique way ... a good painter and a completely original one'. John Piper wrote that 'her paintings ... are of the times and timeless. They are powerful and extraordinary, and are about humanity and its fate.' His wife, Myfanwy Piper, also an art critic, wrote: '[O]ne is overwhelmed by a dazzling live quality. It is not only the beauty of the paintings but the independence and passion of the vision that produced them that is so moving.' Myfanwy Piper was later commissioned to produce a monograph on Hodgkins for The Penguin Modern Painters: a series of short books on 19 individual artists that included Paul Klee, Georges Braque, Edward Hopper, Ben Nicholson, Duncan Grant and Henry Moore. Hodgkins was the only woman artist chosen.

And yet, following her death in a hospital in Dorset in 1947, within a few years Hodgkins had been displaced and then almost completely written out of the record of British art. It was a curious case of cultural amnesia. Actively denigrated in the late 1950s and early 1960s by the new cultural gatekeepers such as Sir John Rothenstein, director of London's Tate Gallery, Hodgkins was regularly omitted from important surveys of British art from the late 1960s on, notably the Barbican Art Gallery's landmark 1987 exhibition A Paradise Lost: The Neo-Romantic imagination in Britain 1935–1955. But Hodgkins was integral to the early Neo-Romantic Movement, painting her landscape mood pieces boldly and independently at a time when most British art was either timidly in thrall to the artistic powerhouse that was Paris, or had withdrawn into nostalgia.

It is clear now that this art historical revisionism—the vaporisation of Frances Hodgkins—was made in order to assert a particular kind of cultural nationalism, with a remaking of the official narrative of British art to represent that. Essentially, her reputation was smothered by British provincialism, where her outsider status and the complex inflection of her aesthetic—with its anti-nostalgia and rejection of geometric abstraction—told against her. The 1960s saw the rise of an International style that asserted the primacy of abstract formalism, alongside the acclamation of hard-edged Pop Art. Artists from the 1930s and 1940s who pioneered similar qualities, such as Ben Nicholson and Barbara Hepworth, were elevated in the canon, while John Piper was anointed both inspiration and prime mover in the Neo-Romantic Movement, despite having been both a disciple and devoted admirer of Hodgkins. The standard art history, British Art Since 1900, written by Frances Spalding and published in 1987, barely mentions Hodgkins, relegating her to the status of an also-ran.

This large new book, Frances Hodgkins: European journeys, consisting of a series of essays by various hands, as well as a plethora of illustrations—paintings, drawings, photographs—is part of a spate of publications about this artist that have appeared since the mid-1990s,

almost entirely from New Zealand publishing houses, seeking to rehabilitate or, latterly, enhance this artist's reputation. This book is also the catalogue for a comprehensive travelling exhibition put together by Auckland Art Gallery Toi o Tāmaki, timed to coincide with the 150th anniversary of the artist's birth.

Led by Mary Kisler, senior curator of International Art at Auckland Art Gallery Toi o Tāmaki, Frances Hodgkins: European journeys—book and exhibition— concentrate on Hodgkins as an expatriate, the indefatigable itinerant who from 1901 onwards travelled in order to evolve as an artist, even at the cost, as she wrote to her mother in 1924, of becoming 'denationalised', one of those who 'have no country'. Hodgkins, the gutsy outdoors painter always en route, was the obsessive colourist, seeking colours to save the world. Colour was her language. But hers was not a confrontational style; instead it was subtle, almost self-effacing: the joy of the eye at what it could see was its own justification, around which colour wove an emotional network of juxtapositions. Hodgkins, a trained pianist, painted as if orchestrating colours into a concerto.

The best account of the life of Frances Hodgkins so far is Joanne Drayton's biography Frances Hodgkins: A private viewing, published by Godwit in 2005, but it is the collected Letters of Frances Hodgkins, edited by Linda Gill and published by Auckland University Press in 1993, that remains indispensable for its passion, descriptive bravura and almost mystical sense of commitment to an artistic vocation. The letters are an account of the growth of a mind out of settler insecurities towards cosmopolitan confidence and self-awareness. Hodgkins in this sense is an exemplary archetype: a Victorian pioneer and accomplished colonial watercolourist born in Dunedin who became an emblematic early-twentieth-century New Woman and ground-breaking modernist painter based in Europe. Myfanwy Piper compared her to Katherine Mansfield, but regarded Hodgkins' artistic achievement, partly because of its longer metamorphic trajectory, as more accomplished.

Over her lifetime Hodgkins produced an almost bewildering variety of work; the recent establishment of the online catalogue *The Complete Frances Hodgkins* provides a comprehensive database. She was a solitary artist of unusual self-possession relentlessly focused on painting *en plein air*, swivelling about her easel with a quicksilvery energy, making something memorable, more often than not, out of the ebb and flow of sunlight over a given landscape. 'Painting,' she wrote, 'reduces me to tears of misery, peaks of ecstasy, depths of disillusion. I feel as if I am possessed of a painting devil which is devouring my body and soul.'

As Mary Kisler records in her companion travelogue *Finding Frances Hodgkins* (Massey University Press, 2019), in which she doggedly retraces the artist's footsteps around Europe and North Africa, Hodgkins was ever a bohemian, permanently penurious, but also footloose and fancy free: 'I am not to be trusted on a Railway Station—the longing to be on board & be off is irresistible.'

Kisler's account of Hodgkins' travel itinerary in *Frances Hodgkins: European journeys*, aided and abetted by Catherine Hammond, is similarly exhaustive, and in the end is a rather relentless chronology of constant toing and froing between fashionable artist colonies in Belgium, Holland, France, Italy, Morocco, Spain, Scotland and Wales. Driving the whole enterprise of recording details great and small, one senses a kind of determined weeding of the undergrowth and overgrowth of international scholarly neglect, and a sleeves-rolled-up burnishing of the shrine of the artist's reputation. In this regard, the most significant contribution to the book isn't from the short essays about specific periods Hodgkins spent in Paris or in St Ives, Cornwall, by Elena Taylor and Julia Waite respectively, incisive and lucid as they are; rather it is the still somewhat tepid praise afforded by British art historian Frances Spalding in her essay 'Frances Hodgkins and British Modernism', placed prominently near the front of the book.

If much of this essay offers a detached retelling of the positive responses of John and Myfanwy Piper, in the end one's impression is that Spalding is still inextricably wedded to the concept of the

Englishness of English art, as extolled by Nicholas Pevsner and other devotees of an almost nativist conception of a full English Neo-Romanticism: one that aligns with the precepts of the Pre-Raphaelites. It's as if Hodgkins remains tainted by association with French influences and lurid Mediterranean colours, whereas for true believers Neo-Romanticism is a pure spring fed by the soft luminous atmospheres of the original English Romantics: John Constable, J.M.W. Turner and Samuel Palmer. What is needed is a larger framework to more exactly place Hodgkins within a world art context, one that compares and contrasts her ability to celebrate different intensities of sunlight and an immensely wide range of colour tones.

In fact Hodgkins was, as Cedric Morris shrewdly observed, 'a completely original talent', in that her influences became a unique composite that she transformed in unexpected ways. If, upon arriving in France in the early 1900s, she 'painted with the eye of a tourist', exposed first hand to the dynamic art movements of the early twentieth century—Post-Impressionism, Cubism, Futurism, Vorticism—she rapidly absorbed them.

Hodgkins began her career with the imagery of a second-hand Romanticism, in watercolour portraits of 'exotic' Māori at Moeraki in the 1890s, but revealed almost immediately an intuitive knack for spontaneity, freshness, an ability to make colours glow—aided by expert tuition from the visiting Italian artist Girolamo Nerli. Later she explained in an interview with an Australian newspaper: 'On leaving New Zealand I went first to England, seeking schooling, but I did not find what I wanted, I was looking for colour and light and I didn't find it.'

But if colour and light were ever her holy grail, it was in Paris before World War I that she learnt to paint landscape not as scenery but as an interior psychological state, combining inwardness and objectivity in the same field of vision. It was also in Paris that she became galvanised by the concept of art as a form of vitalism. In January 1912 she attended the Futurist Symposium at Galerie Bernheim-Jeune, where, among other speakers, she heard the Futurists' leading agent-provocateur Filippo Tommaso Marinetti proclaim from the First Futurist Manifesto: 'The excitement! And the uproar!' she later told a journalist in Adelaide, Australia. From this exposure to Futurist ideas about 'a new art for a new world ... based not on appearances but on sensations' she took a leaf for her own 'manifesto', which she explained to the Australian journalist: 'The student's sole aim is to state his ambitions, to see not with the actual and physical eye, but with the eye of the mind ... Find your sensation and put a line around it.' It was to this injunction that she, in a sense, remained faithful, though as she also put it in a letter to a former student: 'I personally hate all rigid systems—but then I am a rebel.'

Ruia taitea kia tū ko taikākā anake
Strip away the sapwood and leave only the heart
by Anahera Gildea

Pūrākau: Māori myths retold by Māori writers, eds Witi Ihimaera & Witi Hereaka (Penguin Random House, 2019), 400pp, $38

Imagine, if you will, that a great orator is standing to speak. They carry a tokotoko, the symbol of a storyteller that also 'evokes the pou that Tāne may have used to separate his parents' (p. 20). The tokotoko is rapped sharply on the floor, or against the wall, to call the listeners to attention, to wake up their mauri, our mauri, asking us to focus our minds and to sharpen our critical faculties.

Pūrākau: Māori myths retold by Māori writers is a collection of prose and poetry by twenty authors who each in turn have taken up this tokotoko to reconceptualise and contemporise traditional 'storied histories'. Pūrākau, as a form in its own right and as an indigenous methodology for understanding the knowledge handed down by our ancestors, is currently experiencing renewed attention.

As many noted thinkers, educationalists and experts have identified, the word 'pūrākau' itself can illuminate the role and purpose of these stories. The 'pū' is the root, or the origin, or the core of something. It is the seed of the 'rākau' that follows. As the editors mention, this rākau is aligned with the great tree that some narratives tell us Tāne employed to wrench apart his parents. And beyond that the rākau is also an often-employed metaphor for whakapapa. Pūrākau and whakapapa are synonymous. It is this great tree of storied genealogy that holds Ranginui and Papatūānuku apart and allows the world of light, the world of knowledge and *understanding*, to be possible. Pūrākau carry the knowledge of our ancestors, they are whakapapa, our whakapapa, they are our history.

In this sense, the word 'myth' can be both problematic and misleading.

The recent anouncement that New Zealand history is to become a standardised compulsory subject in schools marks a shift in attitude that has been slowly occurring in mainstream thinking across our country. This thinking has been accelerated perhaps by the events in Christchurch on 15 March 2019, and highlighted by the protectors of Ihumātao. The fact that, in our education system, New Zealand history has been largely filtered through a colonised lens is not news, and it has been noted that this movement to deepen the general understanding of colonial impact will also make way for the inclusion of Māori histories. The comprehension and inclusion of a Māori perspective, a Māori world view, has been fought for across multiple disciplines since the arrival of Pākehā. Science has made huge inroads in placing mātauranga Māori alongside Western scientific thinking. The law, educational practices, systems of government, and more, have long been grappling with the need to prise open their narrow institutional frameworks to allow there to be more than a single story.

The word myth, taken from the Greek 'mythos', can be applied to any narrative but it is almost impossible, in my mind, to rid it of the less generous connotations where myth sits in opposition to logic. 'Myth' is commonly understood as a perjorative term commensurate with 'folklore' and aspects of an imagined ancient past that have little or no contemporary relevance and even less scientific merit. They are regularly positioned as antiquated children's stories and in that sense rendered inert.

A quick internal survey will ascertain what level of exposure to 'Māori myths' you may have grown up with at school. Most of us recall the aforementioned wrenching apart of the primal parents, the escapades of Māui who slowed the sun and stole the jawbone of his grandmother and so forth.

The alignment of pūrākau with the concept of myth, whose Western roots are embedded in colonial thought systems, is deeply problematic. I like to think that rather than being simply a story, or a myth, pūrākau is *form*. It is a method of historical storytelling that has particular 'rules' and modes that it follows and expresses. Pūrākau are intended to be educational, to engage the intellect and the emotions, and to be provocative. Traditionally, it was usual to adjust, modernise and retell these histories to make them relevant to their listeners so long as they retained the seed, the 'pū', the core of what the story was about. These were the teachings that carried the value systems of a Māori world view. When missionaries and settler scholars first recorded pūrākau, they were bowdlerised, sanitised and standardised. The storied histories that told of whakapapa, relationships and interconnectedness with nature were routinely amalgamated into 'myths' considered palatable to Western belief systems.

In this time of climate crisis, and movements towards decolonisation, pūrākau are a potential source of inspiration and epistemological knowledge that could redirect our flailing attempts to halt our own demise. No pressure. Perhaps this seems an unnecessary diversion for a simple book review, but given the effect of colonisation on pūrākau, and its subsequent role in destabilising indigenous thinking, intellectual traditions and belief systems, it would be outdated to simply discuss pūrākau as regurgitated or dressed-up 'mythology' without also fundamentally analysing the status of the indigenous knowledge contained within them and questioning how these things are being positioned. These distinctions may seem academic but, as has been famously asked: how do you diminish a culture? You take their language and their stories.

The twenty authors in this book flex their linguistic muscles to give a modern tone to these histories. These are not tidy children's stories that render the world comprehensible and straightforward. They address complex questions and take different perspectives in their interpretations of the 'pū' of our knowledges handed down. The prowess of these reknowned Māori writers is well known and it is exciting that they are able to bring their considerable minds to bear on recontextualising our histories. In times where oral delivery was the only option, and where the tokotoko was forcibly rapped and the storyteller had to sweat to keep us engaged, an audience's agreement or disagreement over whether a version of a pūrākau was accurate, its teachings true, would have been noisy and public. If the story veered too far into imaginative retelling and lost the core of the story, lost the crucial elements of whakapapa, but the storyteller was still engaging and magnificent, it would have been enjoyed, dismissed as pūrākau, but revered it for its status as pakiwaitara. Whether or not each of the stories in this book succeed in representing a Māori world view is equally up for debate, and if the role of pūrākau is to provoke deeper thinking, these stories certainly do that.

Again and again, the tokotoko is raised and this cast of immense orators weave their tales.

When Patricia Grace raps the tokotoko against the wall we can do nothing but listen, as her words are like

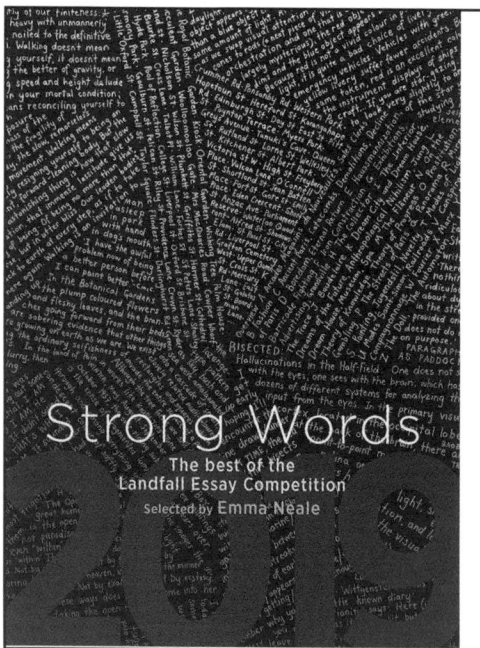

the rolling and unrolling of the tides. In her retelling of the pūrākau Rona in 'Moon Story', we are immediately embedded in the relentlessness of everyday life. There is no high register here; rather we are swept along with recognisable and relatable complaint and irritation. It would be tempting to look at the Rona story as a cautionary tale of a sharp tongue but it conveys far more than that: including that nature has agency and that our enemy is often of our own making.

As Ngāhuia Te Awekōtuku takes up the tokotoko and knocks it on the wooden floor, our heads are brought up sharply to hear the tale of 'Kurangaituku' usually told as the tale of Hatupatu, and our attention turns to consider how human greed and concerns will end in loss. Our understanding of who shoulders responsibility for this is challenged.

When the tap tap of the rākau kōrero comes again, it is Hēmi Kelly with a rendition of 'Rata' that is pūrākau at its most pure. The story of Rata's failure to offer up appropriate karakia is instructional beyond the simple idea of 'taking care of nature'. It is about the interdependence of humankind with the elemental world in which we live and on which we depend. It is a reminder that regardless of whatever justified and righteous ambitions we might hold, our needs cannot take priority over how we interact in the natural world. Kelly's version of this pūrākau reminds us not only of our whakapapa relationship to

nature, but that our wisdom comes from our elders, and our mistakes are not irreparable. It is an exposition of hope and pause and agency.

The percussion of Tāne's descendants continues as Briar Grace-Smith expertly brings us the irrepressible Māui in a post-apocalyptic world, Apirana Taylor and Renée articulate guardianship in a changing world, and the contexts of the stories range across time and space. Frazer Rangihuna's 'Īhe & Her' is nothing short of a revelation and only vies for the most engaging read in this book alongside Kelly Joseph's 'Hinepūkorangi and Uenuku'. The dexterity with which these two storytellers weild the tokotoko is recommendation enough for this book, and I look forward to reading more from them.

Pūrākau is replete with challenges to our understandings of what the core of kōrero tuku iho are. In this moment where compulsory subjects in our schools are being expanded, perhaps it is time to also teach our 'storied histories'. To be equipped and to equip the next generations is the work of our tūpuna— to be able to understand and debate the content of our pūrākau as carriers of knowledge, not simply as wonky fairytales. The pū we plant now are the rākau of our future.

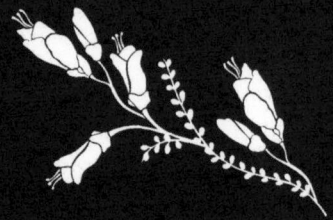

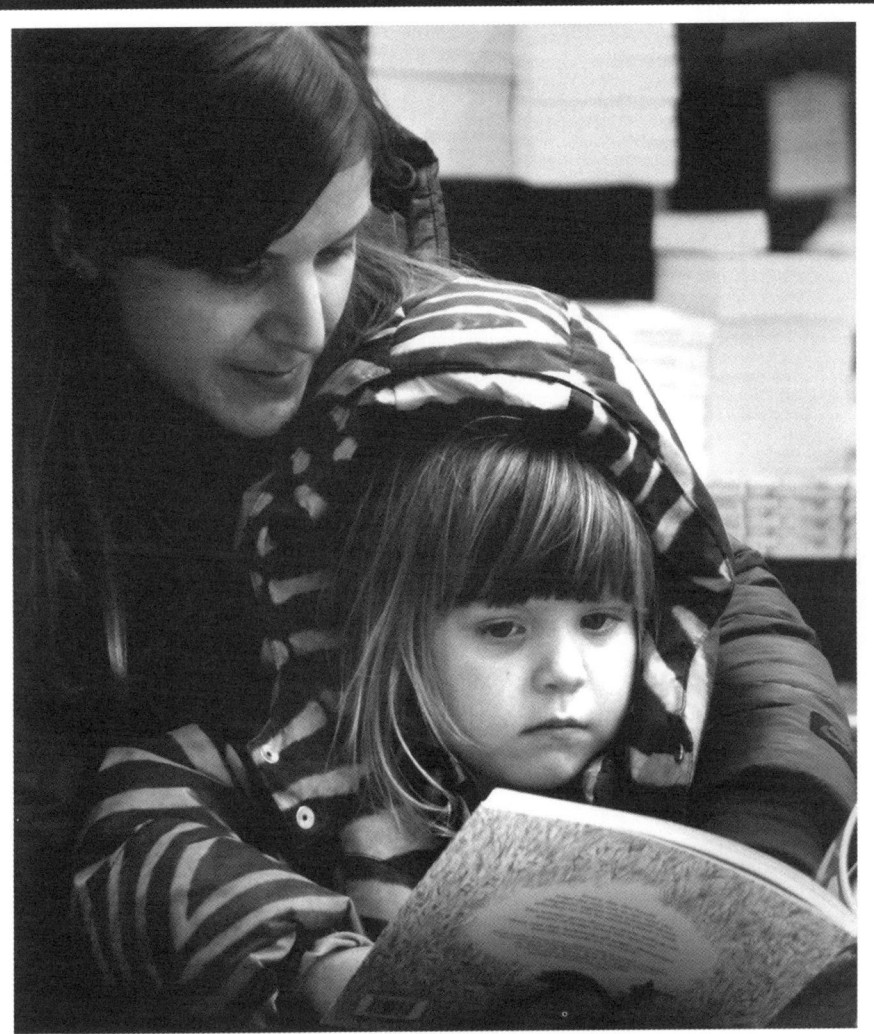

future Landfall editor swots up

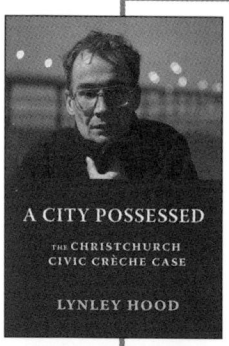

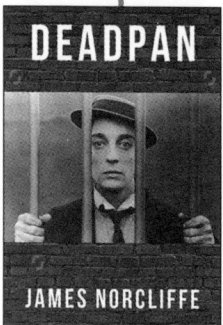

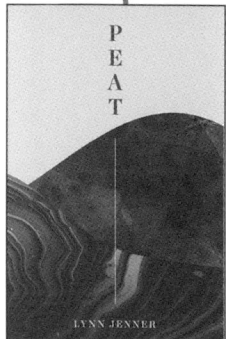

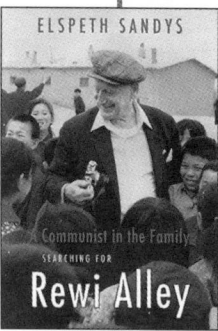

NEW BOOKS FROM
OTAGO

A CITY POSSESSED: THE CHRISTCHURCH CIVIC CRÈCHE CASE

LYNLEY HOOD

Originally published in 2001, A City Possessed is the harrowing account of one of New Zealand's most high-profile criminal cases – a story of child sexual abuse allegations, gender politics and the law. This paperback edition comes at a time when the Christchurch Civic Crèche case has returned to public attention.

ISBN 978-1-98-853185-4, paperback, $49.95

DEADPAN

JAMES NORCLIFFE

The title of James Norcliffe's tenth poetry collection points deftly to the way it conveys big emotions without cracking a smile or shedding a tear. In Deadpan, Norcliffe writes in an alert, compassionate yet sceptical voice. This is the work of a mature and technically astute poet.

ISBN 978-1-98-853175-5, paperback, $27.50

PEAT

LYNN JENNER

Peat starts out as a study of the Kapiti Expressway, built between 2013 and 2017 and passing, at its nearest point, about a kilometre from the author's own house. She decides to create a kind of archive of the construction of this so-called Road of National Significance and begins a quest to find a fellow writer with different sensibilities to help her think about the natural world the road traverses. New Zealand-born poet, editor, art collector and philanthropist Charles Brasch is her choice.

ISBN 978-1-98-853169-4, paperback, $35

A COMMUNIST IN THE FAMILY: SEARCHING FOR REWI ALLEY

ELSPETH SANDYS

A beautifully written multi-layered narrative centred on New Zealander Rewi Alley and his part in the momentous political events of mid-twentieth-century China. Part-biography, part-travel journal, part-literary commentary, A Communist in the Family brings together Alley's story and that of his author cousin, Elspeth Sandys.

ISBN 978-1-98-853160-1, paperback, $40

 OTAGO UNIVERSITY PRESS
From good booksellers or www.otago.ac.nz/press

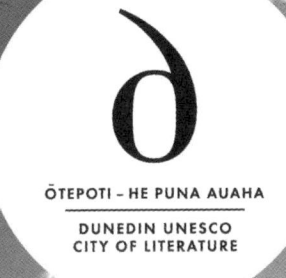

ŌTEPOTI – HE PUNA AUAHA

DUNEDIN UNESCO
CITY OF LITERATURE

www.cityofliterature.co.nz

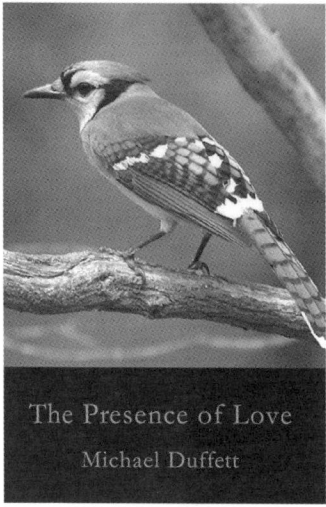
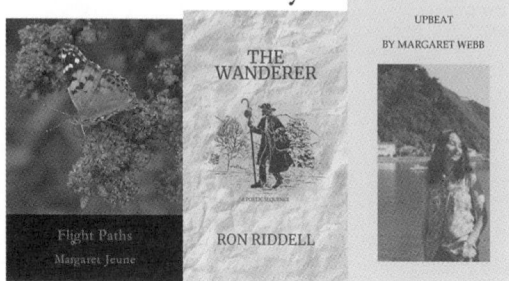
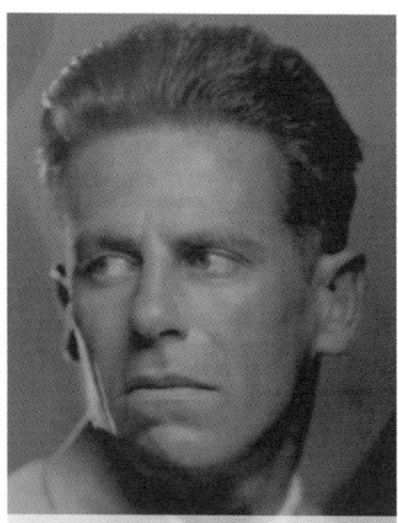

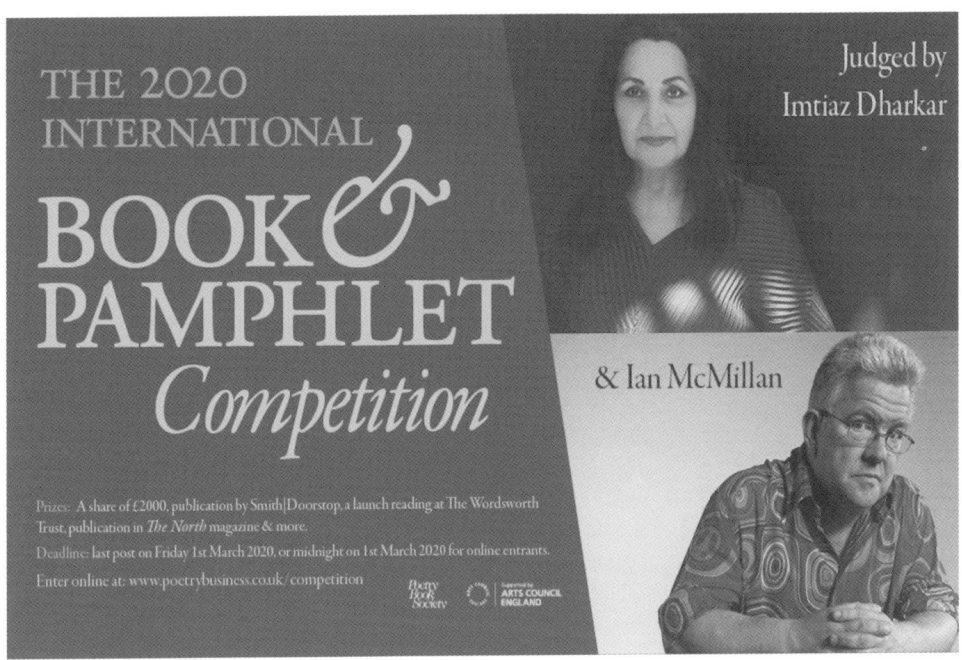

CONTRIBUTORS

John Allison was born in Blenheim in 1950. His poetry has been published extensively in NZ and overseas, including in Landfall 196. He was the featured poet in Poetry New Zealand 14, and is the author of four collections.

Ruth Arnison is the afternoon administrator at Knox College in Dunedin. She is the editor of Poems in the Waiting Room (NZ) and the founder of Lilliput Libraries.

Emma Barnes prefers hearing poems and/or speaking them out loud. She is editing an anthology of takatāpui and/or queer Aotearoa NZ writing to be released by Auckland University Press in 2021.

Pera Barrett is a writer, rapper, IT manager and social entrepreneur who was born and raised in Otaki as part of the iwi confederate of Te Ati Awa ki Whakarongotai, Ngāti Raukawa ki te Tonga and Ngāti Toa rangatira. He is the founder of Shoebox Christmas Wellington and received the New Zealander of the Year Local Hero award in 2019.

Nikki-Lee Birdsey was born in Piha. Her first book, Night As Day, was published by Victoria University Press in 2019. She is a PhD candidate at the International Institute of Modern Letters at Victoria University.

Anna Kate Blair is a writer from Whangarei. She holds a PhD from the University of Cambridge and won the Warren Trust Award for architectural writing in 2017.

Corrina Bland is a 46-year-old learning assistant and mother of two. She lives for poetry, teaching her kids kindness and helping other people's kids learn.

Cindy Botha lives in Tauranga. After a lifetime of reading she's now writing too, and wondering why it took so long.

Steve Braunias is the author of 10 books of non-fiction, including Civilisation: Twenty places at the edge of the world (Awa Press, 2012), The Man Who Ate Lincoln Road (Luncheon Sausage Books, 2017) and The Scene of the Crime (HarperCollins, 2018). He works as a journalist and satirist for the New Zealand Herald, and as literary editor at Newsroom. He lives in Te Atatu.

Liz Breslin writes poems, plays, stories and a fortnightly column for the Otago Daily Times. She feels most alive when her words are aloud.

Mark Broatch is a journalist, critic and the author of four books. He has been a Buddle Findlay Sargeson fellow and a resident at the Michael King Writers Centre.

Nigel Brown is a leading figurative artist based in Dunedin. His work is in a range of mediums. He has collaborated with and referenced a number of poets, and often incorporates his own text in his work.

Tobias Buck studied art history and creative writing at Victoria University of Wellington before completing a postgraduate degree in the US and a master's at the University of Edinburgh.

He has worked in digital media and publishing in London and Auckland, and at independent bookshops in London, Rio and Melbourne. In 2014 he won the BNZ Katherine Mansfield Prize for his story 'Islands in the Stream'.

Paolo Caccioppoli is a chartered accountant living in the Mangaroa Valley near Wellington. He has a master's of philosophy in media studies and wrote these poems as part of a graduate diploma in creative writing at Massey University.

Marisa Cappetta has published in journals and anthologies in NZ and internationally. *How to Tour the World on a Flying Fox* was published by Steele Roberts in 2016, and she has recently completed a second collection.

Janet Charman's *Smoking: The Homoerotic Subtext of Man Alone, a matrixial reading* is available as a free download from www.genrebooks.co.nz. Her latest collection of poems is 仁Surrender (Otago University Press, 2017).

Kay McKenzie Cooke lives in Dunedin. Her present preoccupation, writing-wise, is composing and collecting poems for a fourth collection and editing the manuscript for her novel *Craggan Dhu: Time Will Tell*.

Whitney Cox is a writer based in Whanganui. She completed an MA at the International Institute of Modern Letters, and her work has been published in a number of journals, including *takahē*, *Turbine|Kapohau* and *Headland*.

Holly Craig lives in Auckland. Her work 'Kauri Dieback' is a response to a major NZ environmental issue. A portion of the money from the sale of her drawing will go to NZ Forest & Bird, which is working to spread awareness about the disease. Holly's work is represented by Mike and Linda Geer at Art by the Sea Gallery, Devonport, Auckland.

Mary Cresswell is from Los Angeles and lives on the Kāpiti Coast. Her most recent books are *Fish Stories* (Canterbury University Press, 2015) and *Field Notes* (Mākaro Press, 2017).

Jeni Curtis is a Christchurch writer whose short stories and poetry have appeared in various publications including *takahē*, NZPS anthologies 2014 to 2018, *JAAM*, *Atlanta Review*, *Shot Glass Journal*, *The London Grip*, and the *Poetry New Zealand Yearbook*. She is secretary of the Canterbury Poets Collective, and chair and co-editor (poetry) of *takahē*.

Jodie Dalgleish is a writer, curator and sonic artist living in Luxembourg. She is returning to her own practice after more than a decade curating within NZ's art museum sector. She has been published online and in print in numerous arts-related publications.

K. Day is a poet, playwright and artist based in Ōtepoti Dunedin. They are currently working on a feature screenplay about the stories we tell ourselves, and a collection of short writing about the end of the world.

Breton Dukes lives in Dunedin with his wife and three boys. His third collection of stories will be published by Victoria University Press in 2020.

David Eggleton is a poet, writer and critic who lives in Dunedin. His most recent collection of poetry is *Edgeland and Other Poems* (Otago University Press, 2018).

Johanna Emeney works as a senior tutor in creative writing at Massey University. Her books are *Apple & Tree* (2011), *Family History* (2017) and *The Rise of Autobiographical Medical Poetry and the Medical Humanities* (2018). She is guest-editing the *Poetry New Zealand Yearbook* 2020.

Cerys Fletcher lives in Ōtautahi. She wants to rollerskate places but her mother won't let her. Her life & occasional poetry can be found on Instagram at @cerys_is_tired.

David Geary writes theatre, film and fiction, and is a poet with Pandora's Collective in Vancouver, Canada, where he teaches in Capilano University's Indigenous film programme. He has stories in *Pūrākau: Māori myths retold by Māori writers* (Vintage, 2019), and his play *OWN NOW!* will be performed around the world as part of Climate Change Theatre Action.

Miriama Gemmell (Ngāti Pahauwera, Ngāti Rakaipaaka), when not sunbathing in the comedy duet of decolonisation and motherhood, can be found drawing rainbows in street chalk with her toddler.

Susanna Gendall is a Wellington writer. Her work has appeared in *Sport*, *JAAM*, *takahē Ambit*, *matchbook* and *Geometry*. She has received several prizes for poetry and short fiction.

Anahera Gildea (Ngāti Tukorehe) is a writer, teacher and essayist. Her first book, *Poroporoaki to the Lord My God: Weaving the Via Dolorosa*, was published by Seraph Press in 2016.

Jocelyn Harris was a founding member of the Dunedin Collective for Woman, set up courses on women's literature from the seventeenth to the twentieth century, and worked to promote equal opportunity at the University of Otago. In her latest book, *Satire, Celebrity, and Politics in Jane Austen*, she argues that Austen satirised celebrities up to and including the Prince of Wales, and was therefore sharply political.

Gail Ingram's poetry and short stories have been widely published. Her first book, *Contents Under Pressure*, a novella in poetry, includes two award-winning poems and was published by Pūkeko Publications in 2019. She is a poetry editor for *takahē* and a fiction editor for *Flash Frontier*.

Sam Keenan lives in Wellington. Her work has appeared in *Cordite*, *Landfall* and the *Poetry New Zealand Yearbook*. She was runner-up in the 2017 *Sunday Star Times* Short Story Competition.

Peter Le Baige has published two collections of poetry: *Breakers* (1979) and *Street Hung with Daylit Moon* (1983). During

23 years abroad, mostly in Asia, he continued to write, and returned to Aotearoa in 2012.

Helen Lehndorf is a writer and writing teacher. Her poetry book *The Comforter* was published in 2012 by Seraph Press; her non-fiction book *Write to the Centre* was published in 2016 by Haunui Press.

Emil McAvoy is an artist, art writer and lecturer in Photo Media at Whitecliffe, Auckland. His practice critically examines the cultural roles of artists: as medium, activist, citizen and public intellectual.

Kirstie McKinnon lives, writes and surfs in coastal east Otago. She is inspired by many things: in the case of Lewis— strangeness and discovery in the familiar.

Zoë Meager has a master's degree in creative writing from the University of Auckland, and her short stories have been published and commended at home and abroad. She is fiction editor for *takahē*.

Lissa Moore lives near Palmerston and is a member of East Otago Poets. Her poems have appeared in *Landfall*, *Turbine|Kapohau*, the *Otago Daily Times* and *Strix* (UK).

Margaret Moores is a PhD student in creative writing at Massey University. Her poems and flash fiction have been published in journals and anthologies in NZ and Australia.

Janet Newman had two poems highly commended in the 2018 Caselberg Trust International Poetry Prize. She is a PhD student at Massey University, working on a thesis about NZ's long tradition of ecopoetry.

Rachel O'Neill is a filmmaker, writer and artist based in Te Whanganui-a-Tara. Her debut book *One Human in Height* (Hue & Cry Press) was published in 2013. She was awarded a 2018 SEED Grant (NZWG/NZFC) to develop a feature film and held a 2019 Emerging Writer Residency at the Michael King Writers' Centre.

Claire Orchard's work has appeared in various print and online journals. Her first poetry collection, *Cold Water Cure*, was published by Victoria University Press in 2016.

Bob Orr's latest book, *One Hundred Poems and a Year* (Steele Roberts, 2018) is his ninth collection.

Jenny Powell is a Dunedin poet who has published seven individual and two collaborative collections of poems. Her latest is *South D Poet Lorikeet* (Cold Hub Press, 2017).

Nina Mingya Powles is a poet and writer from Wellington who lives in London. Her poetry publications include *Luminescent* (Seraph Press, 2017) and *field notes on a downpour* (A Leaf Falls Press, 2018). She is currently working on a collection of essays.

Lindsay Rabbitt's manuscript, 'My Mother Was Mrs Central Otago', which consists of poems and four interconnected essays, will be ready for publication in May 2020.

Nicholas Reid is an Auckland historian, poet and book reviewer. He has published two collections of poetry, *The Little Enemy* (2011) and *Mirror World* (2016). He conducts the book-blog Reid's Reader.

Jade Riordan's poetry has appeared in *Cordite Poetry Review*, *Half Mystic Journal*, *The Malahat Review* and elsewhere. She lives north of Canada's 60th parallel and volunteers as a selection committee member (poetry reader) with *Bywords*.

Gillian Roach graduated with a master's of creative writing from AUT in 2016. Gillian won the New Voices – Emerging Poets Competition 2018 and was awarded runner-up in the Kathleen Grattan Prize for a Sequence of Poems 2018.

Shef Rogers is Associate Professor of English at the University of Otago and president of the Society for the History of Authorship, Reading and Publishing (SHARP). He studies eighteenth-century British travel writing and publishing history, as well as NZ book history. He is the editor of *Script & Print* and of the reprint series, *New Zealand Colonial Texts* (www.otago.ac.nz/english-linguistics/ research/publications/index.html).

Paul Schimmel, originally from Aotearoa, is a psychoanalyst and writer living in Sydney. He has published variously, including one book of poems, *Reading the Water* (Steele Roberts, 2016).

Recently **Derek Schulz** has been hard at work, disarranging the haiku form. *Three*

lines/to where/the end begins. He can't stop. Deeply random/certainties/add to the fear.

Elizabeth Smither (MNZM) is a poet, novelist and short story writer. She was the Te Mata Poet Laureate in 2002, and has also received the Prime Minister's Award for Literary Achievement in poetry. In 2018 her poetry collection *Night Horse* won the poetry category of the Ockham New Zealand Book Awards. Her most recent novel is *Loving Sylvie* (Allen & Unwin, 2019).

Michael Steven lives in rural West Auckland. He is the author of the acclaimed *Walking to Jutland Street* (Otago University Press, 2018) and a second volume of poetry, *The Lifers*, is will be published by OUP in early 2020. He was awarded the Creative New Zealand Todd New Writer's Bursary in 2018, and his poems were shortlisted for the 2019 Sarah Broom Poetry Prize.

Chris Stewart lives in Christchurch. His poems have been published in a variety of journals including *Sweet Mammalian*, *Snorkel*, *takahē*, *Aotearotica*, *Brief*, *Blackmail Press* and *Mimicry*.

Robert Sullivan lives in Auckland with Rachel Fenton and their son, Turi. Sullivan's Māori tribal affiliations are to Ngāpuhi and Kāi Tahu. His PhD from the University of Auckland examines the work of five other indigenous Pacific poets. His seven collections of poetry include *Captain Cook in the Underworld*, *Shout Ha! to the Sky* and the best-selling *Star Waka*. He has co-edited three major anthologies of Pacific and Māori poetry. Robert is on the board of the Auckland Writers' Festival.

Stacey Teague (Ngāti Maniapoto) is a Wellington-based poet completing her master's in creative writing at the International Institute of Modern Letters at Victoria University.

Annie Villiers is a published poet and writer who works her day job in Dunedin and lives in Central Otago.

Janet Wainscott writes poetry and essays. Her writing has appeared in various literary magazines and anthologies, including takahē, the Poetry New Zealand Yearbook, NZ Poetry Society anthologies and Shot Glass Journal. She lives near Christchurch.

Louise Wallace is the author of three collections of poetry published by Victoria University Press, most recently Bad Things. She was the 2015 Robert Burns Fellow at the University of Otago, and is the founder and editor of Starling. Louise lives in Dunedin with her husband and their young son.

Maualaivao Albert Wendt is recognised internationally as one of Aotearoa's and the Pacific's major writers. He has published many novels and collections of poetry and short stories.

Iona Winter (Waitaha) lives in Dunedin. Published and anthologised in Aotearoa and internationally, she writes in hybrid forms that explore the space between the written and spoken word.

CONTRIBUTIONS
Landfall publishes poems, stories, excerpts from works of fiction and non-fiction in progress, reviews, articles on the arts, and portfolios by artists. Written submissions must be typed, with an accurate word count on the last page. Email to landfall@otago.ac.nz with 'Landfall submission' in the subject line, or post to the address below.

Visit our website www.otago.ac.nz/press/landfall/index.html for further information.

SUBSCRIPTIONS
Landfall is published in May and November. The subscription rates for 2019 (two issues) are: New Zealand $55 (including GST); Australia $A65; rest of the world $NZ70. Sustaining subscriptions help to support New Zealand's longest running journal of arts and letters, and the writers and artists it showcases. These are in two categories: Friend: between $NZ75 and $NZ125 per year. Patron: $NZ250 and above.

Send subscriptions to Otago University Press, PO Box 56, Dunedin, New Zealand. For enquiries, email landfall@otago.ac.nz or call 64 3 479 8807.

Print ISBN: 978-1-98-853180-9
ePDF ISBN: 978-1-98-859203-9
ISSN 00–23–7930

Copyright © Otago University Press 2019

Published by Otago University Press, Level 1, 398 Cumberland Street, Dunedin, New Zealand.

Typeset by Otago University Press. Printed in New Zealand by Caxton. Published with the assistance of CreativeNZ

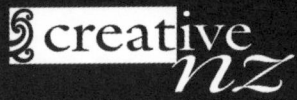

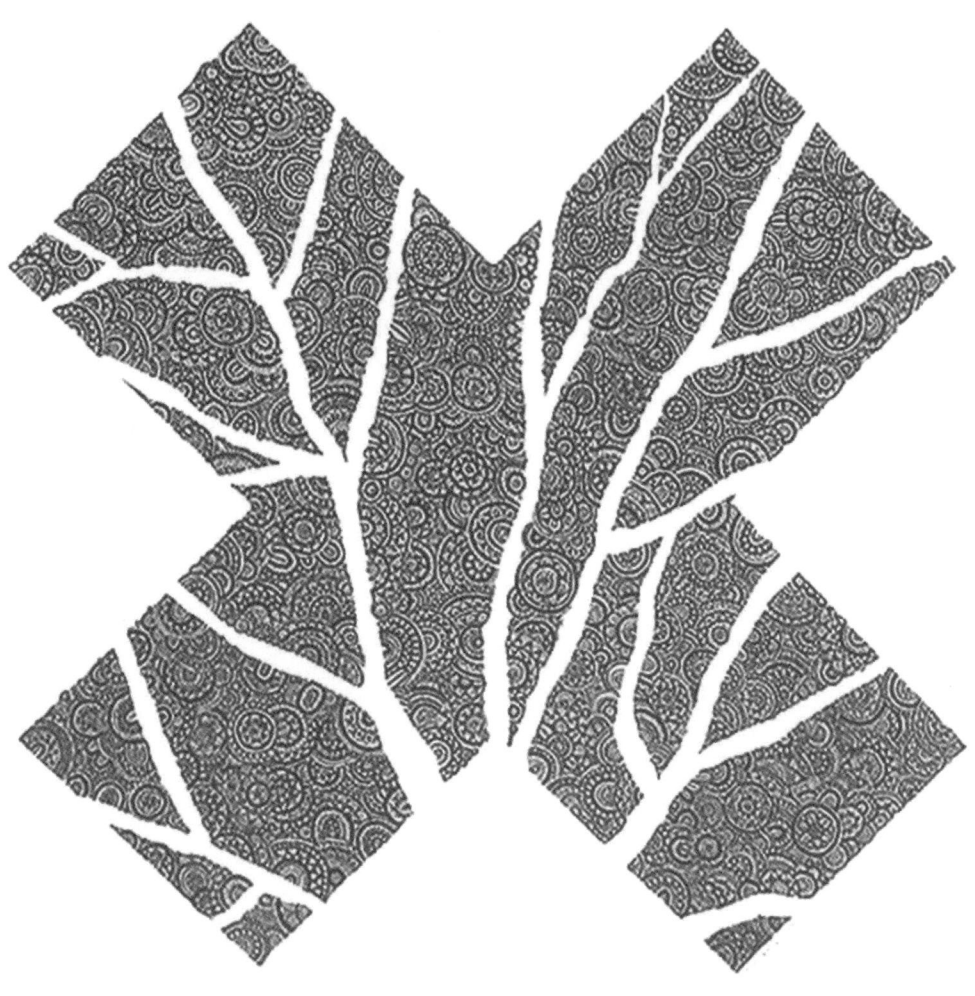

Holly Craig, *Kauri Dieback*, 2019, hand-drawn ink on 350gsm fine-art paper, 96.5 x 68 cm.